Praise for *The Witch's Gui*

"Please believe me: you need this bo__ us who have ever wanted to know more about dealing with spirits, ghosts, entities, and other things that go bump in the night. In the most down-to-earth way possible, J. Allen Cross gives you the prerequisites, orients you to the dynamics, and furnishes you with the practices you need to get your foot in the door with paranormal investigation, improving vibrations in a space, and affecting positive change in the invisible realm. And he presents it all with an encouraging, motivational, 'you've got this' sort of vibe. It's an instant classic: essential reading for all magical practitioners." —**Tess Whitehurst, author of *Magical Housekeeping* and *The Good Energy Book***

"J. Allen Cross uses straightforward and engaging prose to navigate the oftentimes provocative topic of bridging Witchcraft with explorations of the supernatural. Cross's personal experience fuels his take on the basics of Witchcraft, mediumship, paranormal investigation, and, importantly, the practical aspect of working with clients in this field. Powerful and inclusive, *The Witch's Paranormal Handbook* shines with knowledge!" —**Lawren Leo, author of *Horse Magick and Dragonflame***

"*The Witch's Guide to the Paranormal* helps practitioners of all skill levels...utilize their magic and energy work in the paranormal field. By breaking down smoke cleansing, grounding, and how to build their own magic toolkit, J. Allen Cross gives practitioners ways to observe and interact with the unseen world. The ghost hunting field has come a long way in the last twenty years, and *The Witch's Guide to the Paranormal* shows that there are more paths to interacting with spirits than what is seen in modern media." —**Eilfie Music, occultist researcher for A&E's TV show *Paranormal State***

"When you're a Paranerd, you never know when someone might want your help dealing with a ghostly tenant, or trying to get rid of some funky energy that just won't go away, or simply needing an open-minded shoulder to lean on. You don't need to be a practicing witch to benefit from this handbook, and it should definitely be on the shelf of any paranormal investigator who is just beginning their journey into the world of Spirit." —**Patrick Keller, host of** *Big Séance* **podcast**

"J. Allen Cross has written an insightful and unique book on the field of paranormal investigation, which is magical! So many texts have been written on the subject, but none that I am aware of come from the viewpoint of a witch using the tools of the Craft. This book is a must-read for paranormally curious minds, even for non-practitioners like myself. Highly recommended!" —**Jim Harold, host of** *The Paranormal Podcast* **and** *Jim Harold's Campfire*

"Whether you are intrigued with the world of spirits, are a ghost hunter, or are being bothered by a pesky poltergeist, *The Witch's Guide to the Paranormal* is a complete toolkit for accessing the world of the incorporeal. This is the first modern book that I've found that blends a witch's spiritual practice with practical tools for dealing with hauntings. With helpful advice for clearing, cleansing, shielding, communicating with, and eradicating entities, witches will feel empowered to explore the world of ghosts and paranormal investigators will learn traditional techniques for taking charge of spirit interactions. J. Allen Cross has created the perfect book for witchy ghost hunters everywhere." —**Madame Pamita, author of** *Baba Yaga's Book of Witchcraft, The Book of Candle Magic,* **and** *Madame Pamita›s Magical Tarot*

The
Witch's Guide
to the
Paranormal

About the Author

J. Allen Cross (Oregon) is a practicing Folk Witch and paranormal investigator. He serves as psychic-medium and occult specialist on a well-known investigative team out of the Portland metro area. He enjoys working as a consultant for other teams and spiritual workers, exploring haunted and abandoned places, and writing about the paranormal.

To Write to the Author

If you wish to contact the author or would like more information about this book, please write to the author in care of Llewellyn Worldwide Ltd. and we will forward your request. Both the author and the publisher appreciate hearing from you and learning of your enjoyment of this book and how it has helped you. Llewellyn Worldwide Ltd. cannot guarantee that every letter written to the author can be answered, but all will be forwarded. Please write to:

J. Allen Cross
℅ Llewellyn Worldwide
2143 Wooddale Drive
Woodbury, MN 55125-2989
Please enclose a self-addressed stamped envelope for reply,
or $1.00 to cover costs. If outside the U.S.A., enclose
an international postal reply coupon.

Many of Llewellyn's authors have websites with additional information and resources. For more information, please visit our website at http://www.llewellyn.com.

"With helpful advice for clearing, cleansing, shielding, communicating with, and eradicating entities, witches will feel empowered to explore the world of ghosts."—**Madame Pamita**, author of *Baba Yaga's Book of Witchcraft*

The Witch's Guide to the Paranormal

HOW TO INVESTIGATE, COMMUNICATE, AND CLEAR SPIRITS

J. ALLEN CROSS

Llewellyn Publications
Woodbury, Minnesota

FIRST EDITION
Second Printing, 2022

Book design by Christine Ha
Cover design by Shannon McKuhen

Llewellyn Publications is a registered trademark of Llewellyn Worldwide Ltd.

Library of Congress Cataloging-in-Publication Data
Names: Cross, J. Allen, author.
Title: The witch's guide to the paranormal : how to investigate,
   communicate, and clear spirits / J. Allen Cross.
Description: First edition. | Woodbury, Minnesota : Llewellyn Publications,
   2022.
Identifiers: LCCN 2022021676 (print) | LCCN 2022021677 (ebook) | ISBN
   9780738772080 | ISBN 9780738772172 (ebook)
Subjects: LCSH: Parapsychology. | Witches.
Classification: LCC BF1031 .C857 2022 (print) | LCC BF1031 (ebook) | DDC
   133.8—dc23/eng/20220701
LC record available at https://lccn.loc.gov/2022021676
LC ebook record available at https://lccn.loc.gov/2022021677

Llewellyn Worldwide Ltd. does not participate in, endorse, or have any authority or responsibility concerning private business transactions between our authors and the public.

All mail addressed to the author is forwarded but the publisher cannot, unless specifically instructed by the author, give out an address or phone number.

Any internet references contained in this work are current at publication time, but the publisher cannot guarantee that a specific location will continue to be maintained. Please refer to the publisher's website for links to authors' websites and other sources.

Llewellyn Publications
A Division of Llewellyn Worldwide Ltd.
2143 Wooddale Drive
Woodbury, MN 55125-2989
www.llewellyn.com

Printed in the United States of America

To my paranormal team …
You are the bravest, kindest pack of nerds I've ever had the
pleasure of working with. You are my friends, my family,
and my teachers. I am grateful for you every day.

Contents

Exercises & Rituals

Introduction

Everybody's got a ghost story. Just ask around. Even you have probably had an experience that could be classified as "paranormal." It's probably why you picked up this book in the first place. A great deal of folks involved in this work grew up in a haunted home, myself included. In fact, the sheer volume of paranormal disturbances happening across the globe is what prompted me to write this book. There is simply too much work to be done and too few of us doing it.

When I first joined the world of paranormal investigation, I believed that the lessons held in this book were known ubiquitously throughout the community. I thought it must be mandatory for every paranormal investigator to have had a thorough education on all things spiritual that may assist both them and the spirits they study. I was *very* wrong. I began to realize this when folks started contacting me from out of state, asking for assistance. My initial response would be to look up their local paranormal investigation team online and then try to get in contact with them. A startling majority of the time, the response—if any—was, "We can't do anything to help, but we'd love to come take pictures." And that's just not helpful. *The paranormal community needs witches*, and I'm going to teach you how to do what I do.

Within the pages of this book, I will attempt to guide you through three separate but irrevocably intertwined worlds. First will be the world of haunted homes and paranormal investigation. We will discuss the four major categories of haunting: residual, earthbound human, poltergeist, and inhuman entity. We will briefly touch on investigative equipment, protocol, and interpersonal skills for handling clients. Second, we'll enter the world of psychic senses and mediumship. I'll be providing tips for tapping into these abilities and utilizing them throughout an investigation. Third, we'll be discussing the nature of matter and energy as we cross into the world of witchcraft, and I'll supply spiritual techniques to assist you in defending a family from attack and resolving a haunting. These three worlds will be presented to you both separately and together throughout this book, just the way you may find them in the wild. I encourage you to keep an open mind, as some of this work will require you to stray into territory that might be unfamiliar or uncomfortable for some of you. You'll find in some instances that it really is necessary to put aside your personal hang-ups in order to accomplish what needs to be done.

Now, I'm going to say the thing you're not supposed to say: *this work is not for everyone.* If you are the type of person who has to watch paranormal-activity movies through their fingers or who jumps every time the toast pops up, you may want to reconsider making this your path. This work requires you to have nerves of steel and a cool head under pressure. Even if you don't want to do this work for others, I still welcome you to read through this book. Hauntings are extremely common, and you may experience your own one day—and it's good to be prepared. Some of you may even be reading this because you are experiencing a haunting in your home at this very moment. If this is the case, I'm glad that I can be here with you during this time.

If you feel like you are right to take on this work, then you'll want to hold on to this book. This will be your guide and something you'll refer to over and over. These pages cover the bulk of what you will need to know, but I urge you to study everything you can find and speak with other professionals in this field. I've learned some of my most valuable lessons and techniques from other folks participating in this work. Learn something from them, and teach them something too if you can. We all need to work together and know that we are on the same team. Also, listen to their stories. I've been doing this for nearly half of my life, and if there is one thing I've learned, it's that truth is always stranger than fiction. The world is a vast and mysterious place, and we really are connecting with only a small portion of what is out there in our short lives as humans. The spirit world is close, and things do indeed spill over.

So, if you're ready, let's begin.

Witches and the Paranormal

The worlds of paranormal investigation and witchcraft have long been parallel but decidedly separate. We don't really commingle that often, and I think the prejudice comes from both sides. The investigators often like to keep their work "scientific," and that usually means attempting to handle the paranormal with as little supernatural nonsense as possible. On the other hand, witches are often focused on other pursuits and honestly tend to feel they are far beyond the silly ghost hunters they see on television. Despite this, I think that witches and paranormal investigators are meant to work together and that witches have something to offer the world of paranormal investigation that can't be found elsewhere.

Witches work in the realm of vibration. We speak the language of energy, and we know how to move it, mold it, change it, speed it up, and slow it down. This means we can work in the world of spirits and therefore affect them in a way that other folks can't. This makes us particularly good at being able not just to fight off paranormal activity, but to understand it and heal it as well.

For too long, witches have sat on the sidelines of paranormal investigation work. The time has come to enter the fray. The hard part is, you can't just jump from witchcraft to paranormal investigation without the proper education. You must understand the mechanics of a haunting and what exactly it is you are facing. Otherwise, you'll be in over your head in two seconds flat. That's where this book comes in. I will guide you through the finer points of how these phenomena seem to work and give you my tried-and-true methods for dealing with them. Once you have a firm grasp on the mechanics, you can branch out and develop some of your own techniques and add to the tradition of this work.

The Truth

Every single person engaged in paranormal work around the world shares one very important commonality: we are all searching for the truth. Some think they'll find the truth in scientific data. Others think it resides in human experience. Some aren't looking at all, and instead claim to have found it already. They'll give exact answers when they really have no idea, or no evidence to support their claims. Usually, they are easy to believe, because they speak with such confidence it's sometimes hard to catch what's missing. So, the question is, who knows the truth? Who has all the answers?

No one.

No one really knows how any of this works.

Does that startle you? Does it make you second-guess this work? It shouldn't. This is, after all, the only long-held truth in paranormal work. No one really knows what is going on. Now, we've been able to hypothesize about the "other side" and the nature of hauntings based on our interactions with the phenomena. This means that our interpretations may be very close to the real truth, but we will never know for sure. Until we can create some special phone that lets us talk with the other side and get our questions answered clearly, in real time and without any interference, we will never know. Yes, even if we are psychic and can communicate with the dead, our perception is still colored by our conscious mind. Our fleeting personal experiences with the other side are all we have available to try to piece together an accurate depiction. It's a little like if you stuck your hand in a dark box and felt something prickly. Some will confidently say, "That's a hedgehog," and others will declare, "It's a pincushion!" While the object in the box was really a hairbrush, both statements accurately described the *experience* of the object. That last part is the most important: "accurately described." In modern-day spiritual work, it's common for folks to hear statements like "No one really knows" and take that as license to make up whatever they want, but that's not how this works. We should strive for as close to accurate as we can, based on our experiences in the field.

This idea that no one knows the exact truth—myself included—needs to be gripped firmly during this work. It is this understanding that keeps us grounded, curious, and open to the infinite possibilities. It will also help protect you from being taken for a ride by a paranormal know-it-all with bad info. The moment you think you know everything is the moment you should quit this work.

CHAPTER 1
Witchcraft Basics

I get asked a lot if witchcraft can affect spirits and ghosts. The answer, quite simply, is *yes*. After all, witchcraft is the process of moving energy and causing shifts in the spiritual plane. We may not be able to reach out and grab or tackle a spirit the way we would in the physical world, but by casting spells, we are able to play on their field and therefore have an almost physical impact on them. Granted, they have the home-field advantage, but I've found if you know what you're doing and have the right tools, you can make up the difference rather quickly.

If you've picked up a book like this, I'm going to assume that you are not new to the Craft. If you are, however, I recommend also picking up some beginner books and getting acquainted with the Craft. This work is dangerous, and you don't want to be trying a new skill for the first time when faced with an aggressive entity. While this book is good for paranormal beginners, it is not meant to be a complete introduction to witchcraft. Be that as it may, I will be covering some of the "must-know" information here to make sure we are all on the same page.

Mental Magic

Modern popular magic is heavily dependent on tools. Fancy figural candles, shiny crystals, and jewel-encrusted daggers run amok. I think this has happened because casting a spell with nothing but your force of will is not something that can be captured and posted on social media. A great deal of the magic in this book is what we call "mental magic," which is cast with the power of the mind through strong intention, focused visualization, and an iron will. With nothing but our minds, we will be manipulating portals, erecting psychic barriers, and much more. This is where the rubber meets the road and where we separate the real ones from the fakes. Any real witch worth their salt can bend reality and influence the energy of any space or situation with just their will. This means that a good portion of this work is highly customizable. If you're nervous, don't be. I'll be walking you through it as we go.

Intention

I'm a firm believer that intention is *not* everything in witchcraft. However, most of the work in this book will be done with very few tools and a whole lot of willpower. This means that focus and clear direction will be the keys to producing successful results. Before you attempt to do any of the techniques in this book, be sure to pause and make sure you have a firm understanding of exactly what it is you are about to do. We call this "forming an intention." If you are distracted or not entirely crystal clear about what it is you are trying to accomplish, the magic will be weak and the spell most likely won't hold up for longer than a few seconds. So, take a moment and ask yourself, "What do I want to accomplish here?" Remember that your intention should be short and clear. "I close this portal through all timelines and dimensions" or "I banish negative energy from this room" are good, stout intentions. They are specific, but not too long. They're also in the present tense and in the affirmative. "I hope this works" is not a clear or strong intention.

Intention is essentially the blueprint for what you want done. As such, the things you add or subtract from your intention will influence the programming of any spell. For instance, you may intend to close a portal forever, or you may intend to close a portal for a day. These differences matter in your spellwork, and something as small as changing the wording of the intention can change the outcome of the spell. This allows for greater wiggle room in the work. The best rule of intention setting is to keep it precise: short, sweet, and to the point.

The Power of Will

Without tools, you will have to fuel your magic with your own personal will. This skill comes easily to some folks but may be harder for others. Like all things in this book, it'll certainly take practice. After you've formed your clear intention, you'll have to ignite it with the power of will. This is done first by deeply wanting your intention to come to fruition. It's then followed by believing that it not only is possible but is currently happening through sheer force of determination. The intensity of your desire and belief, wielded with a firm and unrelenting hand, gives you the power of will.

If you are having trouble, I often tell people to "push from inside" or to push from the space between and slightly above the eyes while they focus on what they want to accomplish. This helps to activate the strength of your will. Some ghosts and spirits that you run across can indeed be banished simply by willing them to be sent away, and some entities may be torn limb from limb by using just your will—but remember, you must walk before you can run.

Will and intention coming together is also what is going to empower your tools. If your will and intention are weak or unclear, the power of your tools will be as well. It's common to see folks declare things like, "Evil spirits aren't afraid of sage!" My response to that is, "Well, clearly you aren't using it right!" You must put force behind the tools and *use* them. For example, say you are carrying a self-defense weapon like a stun gun and someone comes up to mug you. Do you just pull the stun gun out of your pocket and hold it and hope the mugger goes away? No! You use it! You turn it on and do what you need to do to get the desired effect. Your spells and tools are the same way. They aren't helpful by just existing; they're helpful because we know how to work them. Don't get me wrong; some tools are better than others. If you have a rubber chicken in your pocket instead of a stun gun, you may be in trouble. But remember, John Dillinger escaped from prison using a wooden gun he carved himself, and he was able to overtake thirty-three jailers and inmates using only the sheer belief that he could. This is the energy you need to have to make this magic work. Even if all you have is a rubber chicken, you need to act and feel like it has the power of a loaded gun. Otherwise, the magic will be flat.

Exercise

GROUNDING

Grounding is the first technique any witch needs to learn. It is the foundation on which all other works are built, and it's one that you'll return to over and over again. In witchcraft, the act of grounding consists of creating an energetic link with the earth. This link serves many purposes: it provides a stabilizing anchor for the spirit, it creates an escape route for any harmful energy to exit through, and it connects you to a source of great power.

To begin, sit or stand with your back straight and your feet flat on the floor. It's best if you can do this outside on the dirt or grass, but anywhere is fine. Close your eyes, take some deep breaths, and come into the present moment, letting go of everything else. Once the mind is calm, begin to visualize yourself growing roots out of the soles of your feet, your ankles, and your lower legs. These roots push down through the floorboards of the room you are in, down through the foundation and into the dirt, where they grab hold. Visualize them slithering easily through the dirt, deeper and deeper into the earth, pushing through the rock, past the water table, and all the way down into the center of the earth, where the roots wrap around the core of the earth. When this happens, you may feel a little jolt as your spirit anchors.

On an inhale, visualize the abundant natural energy of the earth being drawn up through the roots and into your body. On the exhale, release any stagnant or unwelcome energy down through the roots and into the fiery core of the earth for recycling. The earth has a wonderful ability to transform old or negative energy into something useful once more. After all, the earth takes cow poo and makes daisies; it can do the same thing for you. Continue with this inhale-and-exhale cycle of drawing up and releasing energy. When you are done, allow any excess energy to flow down through the roots until it feels balanced, and open your eyes.

Without proper grounding, you are likely to feel overwhelmed when handling strong energies or to exhaust yourself by using your own personal energetic reserves. Do this before all other techniques in this book.

———◆———

Exercise

PSYCHIC SHIELDING

When you do this work, there are several precautions you will certainly want to take. The main one is personal protection, which we will be covering in this chapter. The first step is learning how to create a psychic shield, which will help insulate you against harsh energies, negative witchcraft, and harmful spirits.

To begin, ground yourself firmly, as described above. Once you're grounded, visualize yourself drawing up that good earth energy into your body. On an inhale, visualize all that energy condensing down into a small ball of light in your solar plexus. On the exhale, visualize the energy shooting out into a large sphere around you. Many folks visualize the sphere as being made of white light, which is rather effective. Others like to use blue light, which is good for boundaries. Red is powerful protection, but it can be aggressive. Purple is good for defending against psychic attack. Black is an interesting color to work with, because it will eat whatever tries to get through it, which is excellent, but spending too much time surrounded by this color can be a real downer. Advanced practitioners sometimes make their shields out of other things, such as suits of armor, brick walls, thorny hedges, or reflective mirrors. These are things you can experiment with once you get comfortable with the "hamster ball of light" method.

In my experience, some methods are better than others. I like the light method because it covers ground evenly and the ball of light is easy to maintain. While visualizing rings of fire or thorny hedges can be quite effective, they take a lot of energy to sustain for long periods of time. Not to mention, choosing a shield that is too aggressive may accidentally send the message that you are there to fight. So, unless you have reason to suspect a home has something predatory inside it, your run-of-the-mill psychic shield will be just fine. If later you come across something dangerous, it takes but a moment to turn that sphere of light into a flaming ball of whoop-ass.

Remember, your intention will allow you to program how your shield functions. You may construct shields that block out all external energies, or you may create shields that simply work as filters. The latter is important for psychics who wish to receive information while still being protected. Too harsh of a shield can inadvertently block our psychic senses. Using your intention and visualization, you can dictate which energies you allow in. You can also program how long the shield is supposed to last and when it should fade away. The only limit to the power of the shield is the strength of your intention and imagination.

Auric Maintenance

Auras are fields of energy that naturally surround all people. They are an extension of ourselves and are our first line of defense against spiritual attack. While intentional shielding is beneficial, having a strong intact aura always gives you natural ongoing protection, even without active shielding. However, auras can develop holes or tears that let in nasty energy and spirits. To prevent this and keep our fields strong, we need to do regular maintenance.

Exercise

FIXING UP THE AURA

Holes in the aura come from a few things: they can be caused by an interaction with an angry person who unloads on you, and they can also be caused by psychic or magical attack, or even a lack of self-care or awareness. If we have tears in our aura, we can feel tired, or very raw, like we are energetically sunburned or like everyone's emotions are way too loud. It feels a bit like there is nothing separating you from others. When this happens, we need to spend some time repairing our aura.

To begin, sit comfortably and ground yourself. Take some slow, deep breaths and close your eyes. Tune into the feeling of your aura, and visualize it in your mind if you can. First, notice if there are any colors, and if there are, do they seem friendly? A beautiful magenta streak may feel very loving, and you may want to keep it around. However, if you have a nasty brown spot, a sickly green stripe, or a cloud of black energy that is giving you bad vibes, you will want to take care of that first. Bring your hands to your heart center in prayer position and envision them being engulfed in brilliant white fire. Once that is done, reach out and clear away the things you no longer want in your aura. You may do this by sweeping them away, or you may pluck them out and drop them onto the ground, where they get absorbed into the earth. If anything you're pulling out seems unruly, tie it in a knot—or if you're fancy, a balloon animal. After that, it should be much more agreeable. Disconnect any hooks or odd, tick-like creatures that you may come across as well. Do this gently but confidently. They don't belong there anyway. When you're done, flick your hands toward the ground to rid them of any lingering energy.

Next, take a moment and bring your awareness to the outer edges of your aura. Do you feel any holes, tears, or thin spots? You may be able to see them in your mind's eye, or you may feel them as cold spots, like the hole is letting in a draft. If you come across a hole or tear, cup your hands and visualize a ball of beautiful light forming in them. The light may be white or gold; white is high vibrational but can occasionally be too harsh, and while gold is not as protective, it's very nourishing. At the end of the day, it doesn't matter; experiment and work with your favorite. When you have this ball formed in your hands, gently place it in the hole in your aura and see it melting into place, sealing the aura smoothly, as if nothing was ever wrong. Alternatively, I knew someone once who would sew her aura up with golden thread as a means of repair, and I quite like that imagery.

Exercise

FLUSHING THE AURA

Sometimes we need to flush out our aura and energy system. This is good to do after an investigation to clean everything out. To do this, sit comfortably and ground yourself. Take some deep, slow breaths and close your eyes. Visualize a bright light in the sky, like a massive star high above you, and understand that this is the inexhaustible source of loving and creative energy. See it pour gorgeous white light straight down, like a faucet turning on. Let this light pour in through the top of your head and fill your whole body with radiant light. Once your body has filled, let the light spill out of the top of your head and into your aura. See it fill your aura with healing energy that collects anything that's not supposed to be there. Let the light spill out of the top of your aura, carrying away anything bad and refreshing the energy field. Once your aura has been flushed to your satisfaction, turn off the flow of white light and visualize the outer edge of the field turning to brilliant blue light. This highly protective color helps to seal your aura.

Exercise

STRENGTHENING THE AURA

Did you know that you can build a stronger aura? A strong aura means less chance of tears and stronger passive protection, even when you're not actively shielding. There are many ways to go about this, but one way to do so is to sit comfortably and close your eyes. Take some deep breaths and ground yourself. Bring your awareness to your aura, especially the edges. See the edges rimmed with bright blue light that you bring up from your grounding roots. Imagine the blue light completely surrounding you and pulsating with vibrant energy. Sit with this for a while. The longer you sit with it, the stronger it will be.

Another way of going about this is to visualize golden light pouring down into the crown of your head, as in the exercise above. Let it fill your body and spill out into your aura, where it nourishes and strengthens your energetic field. I think of this one as chicken soup for the aura—makes it strong and healthy. You can also do baths with infusions of protective plants like bay or rue. These plant spirits will help to fortify your aura. Just don't use rue if you are pregnant or trying to become pregnant.

Exercise
SENSING ENERGY

In order to do this work, you'll need to be able to sense subtle energies; otherwise, you'll be flying blind. To practice and develop this skill, I suggest you gather some natural materials like stones or living plants, either in a pot or still in the ground. Small animals can also work, but they tend to be too active and hard to sit still with. You may try this with a human too—just make sure to get consent first, or else it will be real creepy. Once you have your object, whether it is a plant, stone, or person, sit or stand in front of it and close your eyes. Clear your mind and ground yourself. When your mind is quiet, reach out a hand and start about a foot away from the object, and ever so slowly, move closer to the object. You may keep your eyes closed or open; it doesn't matter. Notice any subtle energies, such as pulses, temperature fluctuations, tingling, static, or pressure, as you get nearer to the object. If you close your eyes, does the energy you are sensing have a color? Does it remind you of something else, like the fluttering of a butterfly or the hum of a beehive? There are no right answers at this point, but learning to sense these energies is imperative to this work. I suggest doing this with many different natural objects—bushes and trees, different types of rocks and stones, people, and so on—and see if you can feel any differences among them.

Energy Projection and the Body

In this work, it's helpful to realize that energy is most easily projected from certain places in the body. These places are numerous, but the two most commonly worked with are the "projective" hand and the center of the forehead, just above the space between the eyes. When it comes to projecting energy for seals or the other techniques you will be learning in this book, it can be quite beneficial to "push" from these areas.

When it comes to deciphering which is your projective hand and which is your receptive hand, there are a couple of ways to go about it. Generally, it is believed that your right hand is the projective hand and your left is the receptive. While this makes sense to some degree, folks also tend to overlook left-handed people. If you are left-handed, it's possible that the reverse is true for you, but not in all cases. To test this, sit comfortably and close your eyes. Visualize or focus intently on producing a white flame from each hand in turn. Pay attention to which one seems stronger. Similarly, try the energy-sensing technique above with each hand in turn and see which hand seems to be more receptive. Both hands will be able to do projective and receptive work, but you may come to recognize that each hand has an affinity for one type of work over the other.

Protective Charms

While doing this work, you'll want to carry a protective charm with you. Used in tandem with your psychic shield, this will help keep you safe during investigations. The charm that you choose is largely up to you. It may be a rock or a crystal, a small bag of herbs, or a piece of jewelry with a protective symbol, such as a cross necklace or pentagram ring. Each of these will have different properties and natural strengths and weaknesses, so pick what works best for you. If you are going to be taking on heavier cases with higher risk, I recommend investing in some higher-level protection. Blessed Saint Benedict and Saint Michael medals are nice to have with you, particularly if you intend to handle cases involving malevolent or "demonic" entities. Whatever it is you choose, it will need to be charged and enchanted.

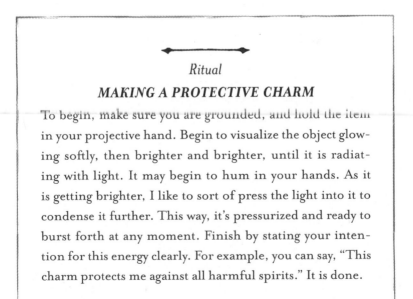

Ritual

MAKING A PROTECTIVE CHARM

To begin, make sure you are grounded, and hold the item in your projective hand. Begin to visualize the object glowing softly, then brighter and brighter, until it is radiating with light. It may begin to hum in your hands. As it is getting brighter, I like to sort of press the light into it to condense it further. This way, it's pressurized and ready to burst forth at any moment. Finish by stating your intention for this energy clearly. For example, you can say, "This charm protects me against all harmful spirits." It is done.

What If I Can't Visualize?

This is a common issue and not something to worry about. Some folks will get better at visualizing with practice, so don't get discouraged if it's hard at first. If, however, you get the feeling after time that your brain just doesn't work that way, it's okay. You may replace visualization with focused power and feeling. For instance, in one of the exercises above, I tell you to visualize your hand engulfed in white fire. Instead of trying to see this in your mind, focus on the *idea*, and let it be true. *Feel* the energy of the flames around your hand. Like visualization, this may be difficult at first, but it gets easier as you go.

CHAPTER 2
Cleansing and Clearing

Cleansing is a broad term. It could mean chasing out the things we think are bad and leaving behind the things we feel are good. It could mean getting rid of everything, including the good, the bad, and everything in between. It might also mean healing a sad memory from a place so it can be released. Before you begin cleansing, you must understand which of these you intend to do. Without this understanding, you may not know which tools to ally yourself with.

This is one of the few places in this book where we will dive into the world of tools and other helpers. Remember, the tools are useful, and some work better than others in certain situations, but the real power comes from combining the right tools with strong will and intention. Think of your tools as a car: you'll want a Jeep for some situations and a Ferrari for others, but neither will do much good if you don't know how to drive.

Before you reach for a tool, ask yourself: What needs to be done? Does something need to be chased away? Does trapped energy need to be unbound? Does a hot room need to be cooled? Does the space need to be made holy? The answers will dictate which methods you choose.

Calling In

When cleansing, folks tend to focus on the banishing portion of the act. This is important, but you may find that this approach

tends to create a bit of a wrestling match with the energy or entities you are trying to exorcise. In order to mitigate this issue, I've
found it's best to simultaneously call in good energies and good
spirits. The arrival of helpful spirits and energies will assist you
by tipping the scales in your favor and shoving out the nastiness.
Their simple presence will lift the energy or vibration of the space,
making it that much harder for dark or lower-level energies and
entities to remain. Remember, you as a living person are powerful,
but you're only one person against a whole host of supernatural
creatures. Having backup is invaluable, especially when it comes to
the heavy lifting.

When I'm doing cleansing work, whether it's with waters,
smoke, or something else, I constantly speak aloud, telling all negative energies that it's time to leave while also calling in positive
beings of light and inviting a divine holy power into the space. I ask
for their help in removing the nasty energies and ask them to settle
and make a home in the space. This often works much better than
just telling the bad stuff to get out.

Change Your Energy, Change the Home's Energy

We have to remember that we are active participants in this work
and that how we feel ourselves will impact the results. If we are
scared, anxious, angry, or unable to let go of some uncomfortable
emotion, the cleansing won't go very well. When we begin the
cleansing process, it is important for us to also allow ourselves to
be cleansed. When you light the incense or begin to sprinkle the
water, relax your shoulders and let go of your own stress the way
you hope the home will let go of what burdens it. This will have an
effect on the space and help the energy release in the way that you

want it to. If you are trying to cleanse away bad energy while you are full of anxiety or stress, you'll simply be dirtying the room as quickly as you are cleaning it, and it will be a lot harder to achieve the desired effect. If you can't let go, neither can the space.

The Direction of Cleansing

Traditionally, most folks will cleanse in a top-to-bottom and back-to-front direction, meaning they will begin on the top floor and work their way to the ground floor, and work from the back door to the front door. The idea here is that you gather up all the bad energy and shove it out the front door. This is quite handy to keep in mind, and I find it works quite well, especially when there is no basement. Generally, the reverse—moving from the front door to the back door—is considered to be bringing things into the home, which can be useful for other types of work.

On the flipside, I have a habit of working bottom to top, from the basement to the top floor. This is not necessarily traditional, but your choice of direction should fit your intention. I often choose working from bottom to top in order to lift the energy of the space with me as I climb from the basement to the top floor, the idea being that I am lifting the blanket of heavy, dark energy up, higher and higher as I go, until it just floats away, relieving the oppressive weight on the home. I also tend to pray profusely while I do this work and feel the act of starting low and moving up helps to bring myself—and therefore the home—closer to a divine source of light, clarity, and healing. Use whichever version makes the most sense to you.

If the home is only one story or an apartment, I will often go back to front or in a counterclockwise manner, but make the call yourself when you get there. You honestly don't have to adhere to any directional rules, especially if they don't make sense or you feel they are overcomplicating the process.

Smoke Cleansing

The first thing people usually reach for when it comes to cleansing is some sort of smoke. Whether performed with incense, herbs, or resins, smoke cleansing calls on the powers of air and fire. The air element is light, uplifting, and adaptable. One of the hallmarks of this approach is its ability to cover ground quickly and evenly. It's easy to fill a room with smoke, and it gets into all the corners and seeps through all the cracks. This means it leaves very few places to hide. Choosing the right incense can dramatically change the energy of a space, which instantly makes this method a favorite. The element of fire involved in this work also has its benefits. Fire is transformative and deeply cleansing. In this instance, fire is also the key that releases the plant spirit from its physical form and transforms it into smoke.

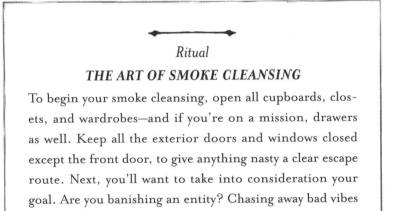

Ritual

THE ART OF SMOKE CLEANSING

To begin your smoke cleansing, open all cupboards, closets, and wardrobes—and if you're on a mission, drawers as well. Keep all the exterior doors and windows closed except the front door, to give anything nasty a clear escape route. Next, you'll want to take into consideration your goal. Are you banishing an entity? Chasing away bad vibes after an argument? Hoping to unbind blocked energy? Knowing exactly what you want to do will help you choose your smoke and help focus your intention. Once you've selected your smoke and declared your intention, you're ready to start.

Cleanse each room by taking your chosen smoke around it in a counterclockwise fashion, to the best of your ability, making sure to stop and smoke each corner. Remember to use your intention to send away the bad and call in the good. You don't have to go overboard with the smoke—just a nice, even haze throughout the home. Also, don't forget to waft the smoke under beds and into crawl spaces and attics. It's common for bad things to try to hide in these places. Smoke cleansing is nice because it allows you to get into all the hard-to-reach spots. I've also found that it's helpful to pray over the plants or resins you'll be using before ignition. Be sure to smoke doorways, windows, mirrors, and other thresholds in the home. Once you've blanketed the home in a thin haze, let it sit like that for a few moments, and then open all doors and windows to bring in fresh air. This act alone can be very helpful, and I recommend that most clients air out their homes frequently to recycle the energy.

Note: Before smoke cleansing, it's polite to ask your clients if they are okay with it, especially if you are going to be using something really smelly. This process can also pose health risks if the clients have asthma or some other condition that may be aggravated by it.

Plant Spirit Allies

All smoke cleansing requires a dried plant ally of some form. Whether it's leaves or branches or bits of resin, these all came from plants at one point or another. Understanding the plant spirits can help you choose which one is best for your situation. Below is a short list of options you may find at your disposal.

Frankincense: This resin is good for chasing away negative entities and lifting the vibrations of a space. When paired with myrrh, it makes what we call "church incense."

Copal: This is another resin, very similar to frankincense, that is excellent for unblocking stagnant energy and lifting the vibrations. This is a sacred resin and should be used sparingly and with respect.

Dragon's Blood: This resin can be rather expensive, but it's quite effective for protection, cleansing, and chasing off nasty entities.

Benzoin: This one pairs well with all of the above resins and has a pleasantly sweet aroma. I like to pair it with dragon's blood to help lighten its energy.

Juniper: The branches of juniper have long been burned to purify a space of evil. This is known to drive out negative entities as well as bad energies and sickness.

Eucalyptus: Just about everyone knows the scent of eucalyptus. It's a powerful cleanser and lifter of vibrations that both repels evil and draws in good spirits.

Camphor: This plant, along with eucalyptus, is what gives Vicks VapoRub its intense, clarifying scent. These days, camphor can be found in small blocks that are usually sold as an alternative to mothballs or to keep tools or silverware from tarnishing. These blocks may be placed on charcoal disks. The heat of the charcoal vaporizes the camphor and produces clouds of very intense cleansing smoke. I lean on this one when I really have something heavy to clear out. Handle this carefully and don't breathe it in. It can burn your lungs and eyes.

Rosemary: This pungent herb is used frequently to clear negativity, lift the energies of a space, promote healing, and bring clarity. Rosemary can be useful when the inhabitants of the space have been facing depression or are otherwise in need of emotional healing. It's a versatile plant, so reach for rosemary when you are unsure what to choose.

Thyme: In ancient times, thyme was burned to purify temples, and it is a great choice for clearing negative energies from a space. I like to pair it with rosemary and a resin like frankincense.

Nag Champa: Yep, even your garden variety nag champa can be used to cleanse a space, unlock trapped memory, and lift the vibration. This is a budget-friendly, easy-to-find option that can be used in many ways. Remember, all things are powerful if we use them with strong will and intention.

Mugwort: Most folks use this plant for enhancing psychic abilities, and while it is great at that, it's also a powerful banishing herb. When burned, this plant will drive out evil spirits and bad energies.

Garlic: In particular, garlic skins are burned on charcoal to drive out negative entities. It's stinky, but it works. Garlic is also highly protective and can be burned around the perimeter of a home after an exorcism to keep anything nasty from returning.

Asafoetida: Also known as "devil's dung," this is an extremely stinky plant. While this is guaranteed to drive out just about anything in the home—including its living human inhabitants—it's also known to remove the good and the bad equally. It will also disempower magical charms and protection in the space. Think of this as a hard reset, and use it only as a last resort.

Red Pepper: Burning a chili pepper on a hot coal is extremely cleansing. However, it's also very harsh on the people who come in contact with it. It's extremely irritating to the eyes and lungs. If you have an intense situation that you feel calls for it, use a *small* amount of dried hot pepper paired with a resin like frankincense or copal, and pray over them both before lighting. When doing this, I often call upon Saint Michael the Archangel.

Water Cleansing

Water cleansing can be done either by itself or in addition to other methods of cleansing. While this can be a substitute for using smoke, these two methods can also be used in tandem. If you follow smoke cleansing with water cleansing, it completes a cycle of heating the space (with fire and smoke) and then cooling the space (with water).

I normally mix up a batch of cleansing water by hand in a white or glass bowl, using a base of cool water. You can choose to use a fancy base, such as spring water, moon water, or something similar, but truly, I simply use cool tap water and it works just fine.

Once you've added in your other ingredients, should you choose to use them, say prayers or words of power over the water and distribute it by flicking the droplets around, either using your hand or a small bundle of fresh, fragrant plants like mint, rosemary, lemon balm, and rue. I will sometimes even use these mixtures as a wash by dipping a cloth in the water and washing down the walls and thresholds for a more controlled cleansing. Some like to put these water mixtures into spray bottles, but that feels less ceremonial to me, so I like to stick with the bowl. Below is a list of ingredients you may mix into your bowl of water to further empower it.

Salt: Salt water is the thing you will probably use the most. Salt is deeply purifying and repels ghosts and evil spirits of all kinds. I prefer to use blessed sea salt (see page 192), but work with what you have.

Floral Water: Floral waters like rose water and orange blossom water have a profound calming effect on a space. If the spirits of a home are unruly or unwilling to cooperate, I find that cooling the area down with rose water or some other floral water really puts them in a better mood, where I can reason with them. These waters are also gently cleansing and good for freshening the energy of a space.

Florida Water: This is a cologne that is used frequently in many forms of folk magic. It has a fresh floral scent, it's deeply cleansing, and it has a very cooling energy. It's like floral waters on steroids. It will also turn the water in the bowl white and cloudy, which has its own merits if you are someone who likes to work with color magic.

Holy Water: Holy water is a favorite of mine, especially when a space needs blessing, healing, or the presence of the Divine. Many folks try to use holy water on the ghosts of dead humans, but this doesn't really work. Humans are not harmed or repelled by holy water, and neither are their ghosts. However, many negative entities will flee from it, as will demons. We must understand, though, that they aren't running from the water itself as much as the presence of the Divine contained within it.

Herbal Water: You may opt to use a water that is infused with herbs in one way or another. Most of the time you will be using a cooled infusion created by boiling the plants in the water, or you may use a dropper to add an herbal tincture to your water base. In either case, you are releasing a plant spirit into liquid form to work with.

You may combine as many or as few of the above ingredients together to get the desired effect. As you go through the home sprinkling the water, I recommend using your finger to draw protective or holy symbols on doorways, windowsills, and even walls around the space with the water. As you do this, declare blessings upon the space and invite holy spirits or beings of light to assist you.

Sound Cleansing

When things are really stuck and it seems like you just can't get the energy moving again, I recommend reaching for something that makes sound. Sound, after all, is a vibration, and it has its own energy that translates to the spirit realm with astounding efficacy. This approach to the work can have a variety of desired effects. It can break up stuck or stagnant energy, bring balance and harmony to unbalanced spaces, unlock trapped energy, and scare away negative entities. In my experience, a variety of sounds will work, but for cleansing and clearing, a high, clear tone is best. If it can't be pretty, it should at least be sharp or startling, such as smashing pots and pans together. Each quality has its own merits. The high, clear tone raises the vibration of a space and promotes healing and clarity. This is unfavorable for negative energies and entities, and they tend to flee. I suspect they experience a high, clear sound on the other side as being extremely bright. Conversely, harsh sounds like pans clanging together can be hard on the energy of the room, but they affect energies and entities a bit like an earthquake. We'll discuss the various tools you may want to use and their efficacy below.

When using sound cleansing, I like to work in a similar pattern as I do when smoke cleansing, by going from room to room and moving counterclockwise, making noise in each corner of every room.

Bells: Bells of all kinds have long been used to scare away evil spirits. I keep a brass one that emits a high, clear tone in my bag and use it frequently in this work. When picking a bell, it's best to do so in person so you can choose the one with the tone that feels the best to you. These can be used to break up stagnant energies, chase off negative entities, and summon benevolent spirits.

Singing Bowls: These have a unique ability to emit long, sustained tones that are very beneficial. Singing bowls can easily blanket a space and harmonize its energies. Their use can be very healing, and they can unlock trapped energy as they raise the vibration of the space.

Pots and Pans: Your garden-variety cookware can be used in a pinch. Whether it's a pair of lids, a spoon and a pot, or whatever you've happened to grab, you can use these to blast apart stuck energy and scare off unruly spirits. These can be quite harsh on the energy of the home, so I wouldn't use this as a normal method of routine cleansing.

Clapping: Most folks wouldn't think that something as simple as clapping could move much energy. However, if I have one goal with this book, it's to teach you that it's not so much *what* you do as much as *how* you do it, and you can indeed accomplish quite a bit by clapping. Just remember to put will and intention behind it. Shake the room with each clap, freeing up the energy and startling unwelcome spirits.

Chimes: Chimes create such beautiful sound, and using them in the home can help clarify the energy. Wind chimes can be hung in problem areas to keep them energetically pure. For tough cases, Tibetan tingsha chimes can be extremely effective. There have been times when the clear *ting* of my bell has turned into a *donk* when faced with some particularly heavy energy. When this is the case, pulling out the tingsha chimes can really get the job done when other sounds can't.

Drums: The deep, resonant sound of a drum can really ground and harmonize a space. Much like singing bowls, the rhythm of a drum can balance the energy and get it moving in a united rhythm. These powerful vibrations can shake loose stuck energy and promote deep healing. Drumming is also a very physical act, which allows us to raise and channel a lot of energy.

Rattles: Rattles can seem a bit strange to folks who are unfamiliar with indigenous cultures, but they can be handy tools. Rattles are simple, but the combination of the sharp sound and the aggressive motion they require, lend striking energies to this instrument. These are often employed to get a spirit to detach from a person, and I've seen spirits react to a rattle the way a person would if they had been punched. Rattles can also shake up and break through stagnant energy.

Fire Cleansing

The powerful, bright, transformative energy of fire proves to be a consistent ally in this work. While the smoke cleansing described above is a branch of fire cleansing, here we will be working directly with the flame. This is, of course, the method you will have to be the most careful with. Fire can get out of control quickly, so please pay attention, and have a plan in case of emergency.

Ritual

WHITE FIRE CLEANSE

This is one of the first methods I learned for removing negative energy from a home. You'll need a heat-safe vessel, something to hold it with (such as an oven mitt), Epsom salts, and rubbing alcohol. You can also use sea salt instead of Epsom salts and can substitute rubbing alcohol with Florida water if you like. Begin by scooping a nice pile of your chosen salt into the vessel and blessing it with a spoken prayer. Pour in just enough of your flammable liquid to soak the salt, but not enough to leave standing liquid in the vessel. Don't go overboard; after some practice, you'll get an idea for how much you'll need to get the job done. Once you're all set up, form your strong intention—such as, "May this fire gather and transmute all negative energy"— and strike a match, dropping it on top of the salt to ignite it and create the holy white fire. Fire is a hungry element and will draw in the energy of the room and then purify it through the salt.

This method is powerful, and placing the dish in the center of a room will cleanse it in moments. However, if you're working with something particularly heavy or dense, I recommend taking the dish and placing it in every corner of the room, going counterclockwise. At each stop, I like to either clap, ring a bell, say a prayer, or do a combination of the above. This helps to unblock the energy, which can then be vacuumed up and cleansed by the white fire. I do this in each room in the home, one at a time. When the fire dies down, you can throw the salt in the trash and start again. When you are done, take the garbage out of the home.

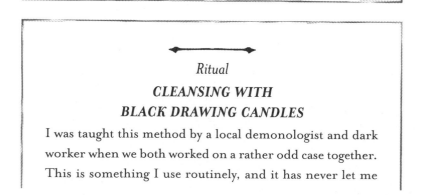

Ritual

CLEANSING WITH
BLACK DRAWING CANDLES

I was taught this method by a local demonologist and dark worker when we both worked on a rather odd case together. This is something I use routinely, and it has never let me down. Black candles have an amazing ability to draw in and trap energy. When hauntings are caused by negative entities, the nasty energy tends to build up all through the house like an infection. These candles act a bit like leeches, pulling the toxic energy out and uprooting the entity. Beyond that, they are really useful as spiritual trash cans. When you are using methods like sound cleansing, after the energy breaks up, it will need some place to go, and having these candles placed about will give you somewhere specific to send the energy.

To begin, cleanse a number of black candles, and inscribe each one with a clockwise spiral starting on the outside and spinning inward, to symbolize the sucking power you want it to have. Finish by speaking your intention over them. I will sometimes make a batch of them on the dark moon and set them aside until I need them (see page 189). When you are ready to use these candles, hold each one in your hand and state your intention to activate its drawing power. Place a number of them safely around the home in sturdy hold ers, and to reduce fire risk, ensure that all pets and children have been removed from the premises. Every time you light one, visualize the candle acting as a vacuum that draws all the dark, negative energy out of the walls, floor, and ceiling of the home. I see it as a black liquid trickling down the walls and across the floor and up into the candle. It is then trapped inside and fed upward into the flame. The number of these candles that you use will depend on the square footage of the home. Each room needs one candle, but larger spaces like big, open living rooms may need two or three, as each candle has a working radius of about fifteen to twenty feet.

Earth Cleansing

Earth cleansing is a much-overlooked method of cleansing. Of all the elements we've discussed so far, this is probably the least impactful method, because the earth element tends to be a slow mover. However, the salt method is amazingly fast and effective. Salt is a potent cleanser capable of purifying a space of negative energy, repelling evil spirits, and bringing clarity.

Ritual
THE SALT METHOD

In my experience, this is best done at the end of a cleansing to dispel any leftover negative vibrations and protect against further haunting trouble. You'll want to begin with a simple salt base. I use coarse sea salt for this. I also recommend blessing your salt with a prayer or words of power.

The next thing you'll want to do is choose an oil. For most cases, simple olive oil will do the trick, as it's all-purpose and great for blessing. You may also choose a condition oil, such as "Fiery Wall of Protection" or "Cast Off Evil," to add some extra power to it. Whichever oil you choose, you'll want to use very little of it; three drops in a bowl of salt is plenty.

The last thing you'll want is some dried plant matter. I would recommend a cleansing or protective plant, such as rue, rosemary, lavender, or vervain. If you are dealing with something really nasty and need this method to have some teeth, you can use garlic or cayenne. Once you have your plant chosen, you're ready to start.

Begin by scooping as much salt as you think you'll need into a small bowl. Bless it, add three drops of your chosen oil to the salt, and begin to stir it. While doing this, I pray, but you may also say an incantation or words of power. As I'm stirring, I slowly begin to sprinkle the dried herb into the salt, mixing it in as I go. To one cup of salt, I would add one spoonful of dried herb.

At the end of the day, using plain salt will still be effective. Again, don't overcomplicate it. In a pinch, using three drops of holy water in a bowl of sea salt will prove to be a formidable combination. Either way, you'll want to take your salt around the home and sprinkle a small pinch in every corner of every room, as well as along windowsills and above doorways. This will purify and protect the space.

The Law of Replacement

Anytime we cleanse, we are removing and releasing energy. This can leave a lot of empty space. Nature, whether supernatural or mundane, abhors a vacuum. This means that something will have to fill that space, and if you don't choose what that new energy is, you leave it up to whatever is floating by at the moment. That's not a good idea, and you may end up in a worse place than where you started. I recommend filling the space with a good energy of your choosing after a cleansing. This can be done in a few ways. You may have a big family dinner with some of your favorite people. You might light aromatherapy candles or incense that makes you happy. You could also play some uplifting music and dance around. Or perhaps you will choose a combination of all of the above—whatever makes the space feel like home.

CHAPTER 3
Mediumship Basics

Psychic ability can manifest in all kinds of ways, including precognition (seeing the future), postcognition (seeing the past), psychometry (sensing through touch), second sight, sudden knowing, and a laundry list of other possible psychic skills. Mediumship is technically a psychic skill, but it's often set apart from the others, as it is specific to communicating with spirits of the dead. Not all psychics are mediums, but all mediums are psychic, as communicating with the dead uses the same mental machinery as any other psychic skill.

While the topic of developing your psychic skills could be an entire book, I hope to give you a crash course in a single chapter. If you are interested in developing your abilities further, there are many books available on this topic, and I highly recommend looking into them. This work requires ongoing education, even beyond what is found in this book. Here we will cover some of the basics to help get you started, as well as some terminology and helpful tips.

Types of Mediumship

Something that most folks don't realize is that mediumship is not just a one-trick pony. There are different types of mediums, different beliefs, and different approaches to the practice. Some seem very simple, others are quite elaborate, and a few are even dangerous. In this book, I will be teaching only the very basics of mental mediumship. However, I want to give you an idea of how deep the mediumship pool really is.

Mental Mediumship

Mental mediumship is the most common form, and it's believed that most folks can do it if given enough practice. These mediums don't go into a trance or speak in voices, and the process often seems very casual. Mental mediumship works through the mental faculties and utilizes the "clairs" (see page 43) to get messages across to the medium. Don't let the "mental" part throw you, though. It's not just messages appearing in your head, although that is part of it. It's also common for mental mediums to see, hear, feel, and even taste spirit messages, yet most mediums report experiencing some of these sensations "in their head." This is the kind of mediumship most often used by television personalities, such as Theresa Caputo from the series *Long Island Medium*.

Evidential Mediumship

This is a form of mental mediumship practiced with the goal of providing irrefutable evidence of the afterlife through very specific messages from the other side. Evidential mediums strive to get information that is so personal that it can't be found online or through other research methods.

Platform Mediumship

This type of mediumship is often practiced in spiritualist churches. Platform mediumship is a style of reading in which the medium stands on a stage or platform and reads for large groups of people. This is also sometimes called a *gallery reading* or a *group reading*.

Rescue Mediumship

The term *rescue medium* is often used to describe someone who primarily focuses their mediumship work on helping earthbound human spirits move on. Many of these souls are in some way trapped or unable to move on, and therefore the help of the medium is considered a "rescue." A great deal of this book will center around this style of work, but I warn you, this topic is quite controversial in the psychic community. Many schools of mediumship teach that there are no such things as trapped or harmful spirits, only dead people and beings of light and love. I know through my own experience this is untrue, but you'll run into it nonetheless.

Trance Mediumship

Trance mediumship is a bit of a bridge between mental mediumship and physical mediumship (see below). This style of mediumship occurs when the reader goes into a deep state of altered consciousness known as a trance. The idea is that the medium sort of goes to sleep or mentally steps aside and allows spirits to come through them and use their body. It's common for people who do trance mediumship to not be aware or conscious during a sitting, and some even come back with no memory of the session. When in trance, these mediums may speak in different voices or accents or take on the different personalities of either their guides or the spirits of the dead they are channeling.

Physical Mediumship

Physical mediumship is a huge undertaking. This is the process of not only channeling spirits through trance mediumship, but doing so in a way that brings forth real physical apparitions. During a sitting, these apparitions may touch participants, play musical instruments, or make sounds through knocking or speaking. While it's believed that most forms of mental mediumship can be accomplished by everyday people, physical mediumship is believed to take a very specific type of person. This work can be dangerous and requires decades of training.

Physical mediumship requires both a medium and a circle, which is a group of dedicated people willing to help. To achieve this intense level of apparition, a lot of energy is required, and the medium can't do it by themselves. Due to this, the circle is equally as important as the medium themselves. Those in the circle are responsible for raising the energy and the vibration in the room, which acts as a bridge between the medium and the spirits. During this process, the medium often sits in what is called a cabinet, a curtained box that helps build and contain the energy.

Sometimes just raising the energy is enough to produce activity like knocking or the movement of objects around the medium. According to some, this minor phenomenon alone qualifies as physical mediumship. However, others say that in traditional physical mediumship, once the medium enters a trance state and the energy is high enough, they begin to produce a substance known as ectoplasm, which is a viscous fluid used by the spirits to take physical form in the room. Ectoplasm is excreted from every opening in the body, including the eyes, ears, nose, mouth, navel, and, yes, the *other* places you are wondering about as well. Once enough ectoplasm has been produced, the spirits may use it to physically interact with our world. It's believed that not everyone is capable of producing ectoplasm, and therefore physical mediums are born, not made. And finding a real physical medium is quite rare.

The Four "Clairs"

Technically, there are many "clairs," but most folks work with the main four: clairvoyance, clairaudience, clairsentience, and claircognizance. Each of these, in order, describes a way in which a person may receive psychic information through sight, sound, feeling, or knowing. Most folks will oscillate between all four but will have one or two that are significantly stronger than the others. For instance, I'm predominantly clairvoyant and clairsentient, but I have my moments with the others as well. You will come to learn yours as you go.

Clairvoyance

Clairvoyance means "clear seeing" and is used to describe people who receive psychic impressions through visual means or pictures. While some see them in real time with their physical eyes, most psychics describe clairvoyance as movies or pictures in their head that play or appear behind the eyes. This is how I experience it as well. Sometimes the two ways of seeing will merge and you'll see something inside your head in real space. For instance, have you ever looked at a blank wall and pictured your family portrait or a poster on it to try to decide where exactly you were going to hang it? It's kind of like that. You aren't really seeing it, but your brain sort of places it there, like an overlay. People who are clairvoyant may also see the future or the past in images or short clips. They may also see faraway places or events.

Clairaudience

Clairaudience means "clear hearing" and is used to describe receiving psychic impressions through sound. Like clairvoyance, people most often hear these sounds with their "psychic" or "inside" ears, meaning it happens in their head. Sometimes, though, clairaudient people will describe the sound as coming from slightly above or behind their ears. One of the members of my team is deaf but is also a clairaudient, so the phenomenon seems to bypass the sensory organs. People who perceive in this manner will sometimes get messages through songs that come into their mind or other symbols, like the sound of traffic or birds chirping. In mediumship, clairaudients may not necessarily see the spirits, but will instead hear them.

Clairsentience

Clairsentience means "clear feeling" and is used to describe receiving psychic impressions through feelings. This is an odd one to describe, because sometimes it comes through as an emotion, and sometimes as a physical sensation, such as pain or pressure. Other times it's much stranger. For instance, I will often *feel* if a spirit is male or female. I will also *feel* that they are blonde, or tall, or I'll get a *feeling* that they wear glasses. What does someone wearing glasses feel like? I have no idea how to describe it, but that's part of the mystery that is clairsentience. It is impossible to describe but can also be startlingly clear for the recipient. Clairsentient people tend to be empaths and may talk about having a "bad feeling" or a "good feeling" about someone or something.

Claircognizance

Claircognizance means "clear knowing," and it's just that: a sudden, inexplicable knowing. The information just sort of appears in claircognizant people's minds like a download. Often these folks won't know *how* they know the information, and they often assume someone must have told them earlier and they forgot. The knowing can sometimes be rather jarring, as it tends to arrive in complete messages as opposed to weird fragments like in the others.

Mindfulness Meditation

Meditation is a key component to psychic development. The ability to calm our mind and not react to new thoughts and information with judgment, doubt, or stress is paramount in this work. When we seize or attach to a thought, the logical and analytical parts of our brain activate, and the psychic parts get drowned out. Similarly, if there is too much chatter, you'll never be able to hear your intuition or psychic senses. Mindfulness meditation teaches us to quiet what is often called our "monkey mind," or the ceaseless chatter that goes on in most of our modern brains. What people don't realize is that the point of this style of meditation is not to do it perfectly, but to *practice*. The act of calmly correcting yourself is the most important part, and practicing this will later help your brain learn to do it on its own.

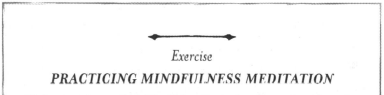

Exercise

PRACTICING MINDFULNESS MEDITATION

To begin, sit comfortably. Take some nice, long, deep breaths and either close your eyes or let your gaze gently rest on a surface somewhere out in front of you. Let go of everything that is not happening right then in that moment. Just focus on breathing and sitting in the room you are in. Stay present, relax, and breathe.

You may realize that your mind begins to drift rather quickly. This is okay. Don't despair. Simply notice that your mind has wandered away and then come back to the present moment. Focus once again on the breathing and try to quiet your mind. Rinse and repeat. Your mind will inevitably wander; this is part of being human. The point is to not get frustrated with yourself. I like to think of the distracting thoughts as bubbles. They may drift up into your mind, but you don't have to seize them and inspect them. Just let them keep floating on by while you stay present. If you find you have wandered away in your thoughts, calling your own name in your head is a great way to bring yourself gently back to the moment. This process of gently leading yourself back to the present moment is the purpose of this style of meditation. Over time, the process will become easier, and you'll be able to sit with a calm mind for longer periods of time.

The Right Headspace

Many books on psychic development and mediumship training will tell you that you must enter a trance state for this work. I don't agree with the use of the word *trance*, simply because it gives the impression that you must fall into a sort of deep sleep or altered consciousness. However, this is not really the case. What you want to achieve instead is low brain activity, and this can be done while completely conscious and lucid. When scientists do brain scans of mental mediums while they read, the mediums' brain activity slows down significantly, especially in the areas that deal with conscious thought, analysis, and judgment. However, when observing mediums during a reading, you would never suspect that their brain activity goes down. They are actively speaking and are often quite animated and full of personality. The idea isn't to fall asleep or disappear; it's simply to make room in your brain for spirits. If you are thinking critically or analyzing the whole process, you are using too much of your brain, and the spirits can't get a word in edgewise. Learning to achieve this state of consciousness is a bit like learning to tune into a very precise radio station. It takes practice, so don't be concerned if you don't get it right away.

Exercise

FINDING THE RIGHT HEADSPACE

In order to enter the right headspace, I recommend sitting comfortably and taking a couple of deep breaths. Relax, and let go of anything that may be happening in your life or happening around you. It's not important if there are dishes in the sink or if you have an appointment later or whatever else your brain may want to fixate on, so let it go. Instead, bring your awareness to your body. How do your hands feel? How do your feet feel inside your shoes? What does your scalp feel like? Choosing one or more parts of the body to tune into can help gather your focus and awareness so that it's not scattered across your whole life. This is a good time to practice grounding (see page 10), which will help stabilize you going forward.

Once you've found a state of calm, set your intention. If you are trying to connect at a haunted location, the intention may be to "safely communicate with the energies in the home." Once you've formed this intention, begin to listen—not just with your ears, but with your whole body. Be open to any sensations, feelings, sounds, smells, mental images, and more. Everyone experiences this in a different way, so it may take a moment to see what your particular strengths are. I mostly get feelings and mental images. You may get sounds and smells. A lot of the time, psychic information comes in a bit like inspiration, or a "light-bulb" moment in which something just comes in seemingly out of nowhere. It's okay if the things you are getting don't make sense to you, because the messages may not be for you, but for someone else.

Making Use of the Mundane

When folks experience spontaneous psychic ability or mediumship, it's often while they are doing mundane, mindless tasks like washing the dishes, taking a shower, or knitting. This is because these activities often put us in the necessary headspace to receive this information. Having an activity may help some people tune into this headspace easier. For instance, I often keep a pad and pen in front of me while I do a reading. It's not for anything fancy, just for scribbling and doodling, which helps me get out of my head and into my body. If you are having a hard time achieving the proper headspace, try distracting yourself with a mundane task like sweeping or folding laundry. If the connection seems to fade in and out, this is normal and is a sign that your analytical mind may be getting too active; try to let go of things like worry and attachment to the outcome and instead make room for spirits to speak. If you struggle with this, try to listen from your heart instead of your head. Even though we call it "mental" mediumship, a great deal of the messages come through the heart space.

In my experience, there is also a noticeable difference in the reading when I'm grounded versus when I'm not. When I skip grounding, the images and messages often come too quickly and can feel very chaotic and overwhelming. It can be hard to separate and identify the symbols. When grounded, though, I feel much more in control, and the reading is often much clearer and less turbulent.

Understanding the Symbol System

Communication requires a great deal of effort and energy from spirits, even when they are working through a medium. Therefore, to conserve their strength, they will often communicate in symbols. This way, they can say a lot with very little, but these symbols will often need to be interpreted by the medium. For instance, if I'm in a building and I hear children laughing, it's my symbol that the place was important to children, like it used to be a school or an orphanage. Pretty straightforward, right? Not always. If a spirit shows you an orange, it may mean they worked with produce, but it may also be a symbol for Florida, or Orange County, or a sunny disposition they had in life.

Spirits will also use your memories, because these are already recognizable to you. For instance, they may show you your third-grade teacher. This doesn't mean the spirit *is* your former teacher, but they might be trying to communicate that *they* were a teacher in life. In my readings, spirits will often show up as famous people who I am familiar with. For instance, I was reading for a friend and the actress Virginia Madsen appeared at the table. Last I checked, Virginia Madsen is still alive, so clearly it wasn't her. However, if I described Virginia Madsen—female, blonde, Caucasian, curly hair, pretty—I would be accurately describing their friend who died, who was a "Virginia Madsen type." Similarly, when a spirit shows up as the person I'm reading for, it's my symbol that the person gets told that they look like this spirit a lot, such as an uncanny mother-daughter resemblance. You may also perceive other symbols, such as an anchor to show that they enjoyed nautical activities or served in the navy. The spirit may cover their mouth with their hand to show you that they were unable to speak near the end or that they took many secrets to their grave. Some symbols will have more than one meaning, and keeping a journal of your symbols can help you get to know the process of interpreting them.

Reading a Home

In my experience, reading a home is much different from reading for a client or group with the purpose of passing on messages from their deceased loved ones. I think the reason for this is twofold. First, I think connecting with earthbound human spirits is much different from contacting human spirits who have passed through the light to the realm beyond. Personally, I find it easier to pick up and receive information from earthbounds than from those that have crossed—they seem farther away. Second, when trying to connect with someone's deceased loved ones, there is heavy expectation and emotional energy placed on the reading, which can prove to be an obstacle for some. Because this book is about haunted homes, we will be focusing mainly on doing mediumship readings for the home itself. Below you will find my tips to make this process easier.

Before starting every house reading, you should have a short chat with your clients. Let them know you will be roaming around their home and make sure they are okay with that. Also, find out if there are any restrictions or rooms they want you to stay out of. Once you're finished talking with them, get started by taking a few deep breaths, grounding yourself, and tuning into the correct headspace to receive messages from the other side. From there, I suggest the following:

Let Your Psychic Intuition Take the Lead

When I read a home, I put my psychic self in the driver's seat. This often looks like letting my intuition dictate where in the house to go and when. You'll want to check out the entire house, but notice if you feel the need to start somewhere. By simply listening to this inner guidance, it will help you engage your psychic senses. So, if you feel a pull to check out the upstairs first, listen to that. Or you may hear a voice that says to look in the basement. Follow your intuition, and let it guide you. Your job here is to be a casual observer from the back seat. Surrender to the process.

Pause in the "Weird" Places

As you go through the home, pause and spend time in any areas that feel "weird." Psychic sense will feel different to each person, but you may find a room that seems to buzz or have the feeling of static in the air. Alternatively, a room may feel very heavy or like it's hard to breathe in. Some rooms will feel emotional and may give you a strong sense of anger or sadness. Others will make your hair stand on end. Sit in these places and tune into these odd feelings and see if you can pick up anything else. Are you getting a picture? Hearing a word? Sensing a presence? If the last, what does the presence seem to be? Lean into the "weird" feelings and see what they have to tell you.

Go Back in Time

Sometimes you'll get the sense that something happened in a particular area, but you can't quite make it out. In this case, I like to stand squarely in the area that is giving me trouble and pretend I'm hitting rewind. This can help me more easily get images or pick up information about things that happened in the past. Depending on how far back you go, you may be able to build a bit of a timeline of events.

Don't Be Afraid to Touch

While touching of personal property can get dicey, touching of the actual home itself can be helpful when picking up on its vibration. This can be walls, doorframes, doors, doorknobs, beams, and anything else in the home that is built into the structure itself. Through touch, we can better connect with the energy of the space and potentially pick up on deeper information than what is on the surface. Similarly, if there is something like a chair that belonged to the former owner of the home that I'm trying to connect with, I will sit in the chair.

Separate the Layers

People often think that hauntings are straightforward, but often they are quite complex and contain many layers. These can be memories of events that accumulated over time, such as the fact that the home was a funeral parlor from 1922 to 1935, and then a murder took place there in 1977, followed by heavy drug use that happened in the home between 1995 and 1998. These events are unrelated except for the fact that they all happened in the same location, creating layers of energy that may be echoing throughout the home or otherwise lending themselves to the haunting.

Alternatively, multiple hauntings may layer upon themselves. You may find a couple of earthbound human spirits in the home, as well as a residual haunting and an inhuman entity. These will all feel different, and it's important to separate which is which and keep track of them. I often do my walk-throughs with a notepad for this purpose. You may also find that the land has a different haunting or spiritual issue than the home itself. Understanding, separating, and organizing the layers as you go will help you develop the whole story and the bigger picture of what you are dealing with. It will also let you know what steps you will need to take to address the haunting.

Remember, though, that this is a skill that takes time. When first starting, go slow and focus on one thing at a time. Don't try to read it all at once. Eventually, you'll get this psychic juggling act down.

Practice, Practice, Practice

Mediumship simply takes time and practice. I highly recommend going to haunted locations in your area that you don't know the real backstory to. Take some time there and see what you pick up, and then when you get home, do some research and see what you can validate. Better yet, have a friend dig up some interesting locations and go with them to the site without them telling you where you're going or why it's special. When you get there, tell them what you sense, and they can tell you if you are correct or not. This was how I got onto my paranormal investigation team. My audition consisted of being taken into the basement of a bar in North Portland that I had never been to before. There they gave me some time to walk around, and then I told them about the history of the place based on what I was sensing. I was right on almost every account and was welcomed to the team.

Reading a Home from a Distance

An exercise we do on my paranormal investigation team is something we call "pre-impressions." This is essentially getting a feel for the haunting, home, and family before even arriving at the home. To do this, I prefer to use pictures. I recommend working with at least one photo of the exterior of the home, as well as several pictures of the inside of the home. While you can do this from a device such as a computer or a phone, I recommend printing them when you're first getting started, as the ability to physically touch the photos can help.

To begin, I like to start with the exterior photo. You may place your hand on it or run your fingertips across the picture to pick up the vibration, or you can simply look at it and see how it makes you feel. Does it seem to emit a sound, or a feeling, or a vibration? If it does, try to tune into whatever energy it is giving off. From there, the exterior photo may begin speaking to you or showing you things like a figure in a window. The trick is not to look for anomalies in the photo itself but instead to feel for them energetically. I don't often look too hard at the details in the photo; instead, I sort of look in its direction with a soft gaze and wait. If the exterior photo doesn't seem to be speaking to you, move on to the interior photos. Don't spend too long on a photo if it isn't giving you any information. I like to flip through them rather quickly until one stops me or gives me pause. Then I sit with it and look at it and see what it has to say. Once I'm done with it, I may go back to the other photos and see if they are feeling chatty yet. Take your time, but don't stay in a stuck spot too long. This leads to frustration, which can make the act of psychic sensing much harder.

Pendulum Dowsing

When I teach this work, I often get some folks who are worried that they lack the psychic skill necessary to do what I do. When I say things like, "I sensed there was a portal in the upstairs bedroom," they think to themselves, "Well, I can't do that, so this work isn't for me." But that's not entirely true. Sure, some of you reading this will have the psychic prowess to do most of this work without assistance. However, many more of you will not have those natural abilities, but that doesn't mean you can't do this work too. We can sort of hack the psychic part by learning dowsing.

Pendulum dowsing is a simple method of divination that will give you yes, no, and maybe answers. This becomes invaluable when you need to identify things like portal locations or entities that are present. For instance, if you suspect there is a portal, you can go from room to room and ask the pendulum, "Is there a portal in this room?" and it will let you know if there is one. If it says yes, you can then ask further questions until you narrow it down to the exact location, such as, "Is it in this half of the room?" You may use the pendulum as your sole source of psychic information, or you may use it to supplement your psychic intuition when you get stuck. I always recommend a combo, because it is possible for entities to influence the pendulum, so always work in tandem with your gut instinct. The more you use the pendulum, the stronger your intuition will become, and you may eventually find you don't need it anymore.

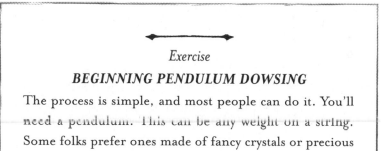

Exercise

BEGINNING PENDULUM DOWSING

The process is simple, and most people can do it. You'll need a pendulum. This can be any weight on a string. Some folks prefer ones made of fancy crystals or precious metals, but I've used my car keys hanging from a length of dental floss. You'll find what works for you. Hold the string loosely in your dominant hand and place your other hand underneath the pendulum, palm up. Some people will tell you things like, "Pendulums swing back and forth for no and side to side for yes." While that may be true for them, I find that different people and different pendulums will provide different answers. So, I recommend starting by asking it to show you "Yes" and then "No" and finally "I don't know" and seeing how the pendulum responds. Try to hold as still as possible, but avoid going too rigid. The pendulum may not move for some time, but keep asking in your mind and eventually the pendulum will begin to move. Remember to set your intention to connect with your personal intuition or "higher self" through the pendulum. That way, you are having a conversation with yourself and not something else.

Selecting a Pendulum

You can find pendulums at just about any New Age or occult store, either in person or online. There are many different types, but most are made out of crystals, usually some sort of quartz or amethyst. I prefer to use clear quartz, as it really focuses the energy nicely. However, you should go with the materials that you feel called to. You can also get ones that are made of metal, orgonite, or even objects like keys. Some pendulums are chambered, meaning you can put things inside of them, such as herbs, waters, or personal concerns like hair or blood. This type can be really versatile and interesting, but for this work they are often unnecessary. Just remember not to get too caught up in the materials. Any weight on a string will do at the end of the day.

Getting to Know a New Pendulum

When you first bring home a new pendulum, you'll want to cleanse it. The method should be dictated by the materials it is made of. Some stones and metals can withstand a soak in a bowl of salt water. Others will need to be held in some cleansing incense or set in a patch of sunlight. Do your research on the materials involved to decide on the best method. Once the pendulum is cleansed, you'll want to spend about a week, maybe two, getting to know it. I know that statement probably sounds weird, but all things have a spirit, and this includes your pendulum. Each pendulum will have a slightly different personality and will communicate in different ways. I suggest always keeping it with you for the first week or so and sleeping with it under your pillow. Over the course of this introductory period, I recommend asking the pendulum several questions a day to see how it responds. This will help you get to know its personal language.

Calibrating Your Pendulum

Sometimes we need to be sure that we aren't unwittingly influencing the pendulum by moving our hand to get the correct answer. First, be sure that after you ask a question, you are letting the pendulum answer. Let your mind go blank and wait for the swing to tell you. If you have trouble going blank, focus on the question, and not the answer while the pendulum deliberates. If you ask a question and then immediately focus your mind on "Please say yes! Please say yes!" then it will say yes.

A good way to practice this is to calibrate the pendulum using playing cards. Start by shuffling the deck and then dealing a card facedown without looking at it. Using your pendulum, you can hang it over the card and ask if the card is red. If it says yes, turn the card over and check. If it says no, ask if the card is black and see what it says. In theory, the pendulum should always be right, but it may take you a few tries to get it in sync. So, if it doesn't immediately get the answer right, stick with it until the accuracy increases to a reliable level. If it's really off, cleanse it, bless it in your preferred manner, and try again.

Staying Protected While Dowsing

Your pendulum can be used to connect both with your higher self or your innate intuition as well as with guides or spirits from the other side. When you use your pendulum, be sure to ground yourself and put on your psychic protection (see chapter 1); this helps keep the connection clear. Also be sure to use strong, clear intention to specify who or what you are tapping into with the pendulum. Do you want the spirit to answer? Or do you want your own inner knowing to answer? Different situations may require you to use one or the other, so be certain to specify what it is you are choosing to connect with through the pendulum.

CHAPTER 4

Paranormal Investigation Basics

O ne thing I want you to focus on while doing this work is helping those in need. The world of paranormal investigation has
its own politics and its fair share of egos, but do your best to not
lose sight of what is important. Each of us will be brought to this
work for different reasons, but making a positive impact should be
at the forefront of everything you do. How you do this will depend
on your chosen methods of working and your personal goals.
When approaching the field of paranormal investigation, you'll
often find that it is split into two different kinds of participants: the
"scientific" folks and the "spiritual" folks. Both are valid and have
their strengths and weaknesses, but the point is to try to strike a
balance between the grounded scientific approach and the open-
minded spiritual approach and to use them both to help people as
much as you can.

But first, we must ask ourselves an important question: "Why
are we here?" Everyone has their own reason for joining the world
of paranormal investigation, and the answers will range wildly.
The important thing is to know why *you specifically* are here. The
answer to this question will dictate many of the choices you make
from this point forward. Are you here because you need a hobby?
Are you looking for proof of the afterlife? Are you simply wanting
to help folks? Take a second and find your reason. Over the years,
this reason may or may not change. However, being in tune with

your own personal "why" will guide you, not only in choosing how to investigate, but where and with whom. If you decide to join or start a paranormal investigation team, you'll want to make sure that the team is made up of folks with the same goal.

Investigator's Code of Ethics

Before we begin, I'd like to go over a short list of rules to abide by when investigating to make sure your investigations are always ethical.

Always Seek the Truth: This means not slapping an unsupported explanation on something just so you can say, "Case closed." It also means not jumping to unsupported supernatural conclusions. Always seek the truth and find evidence to help you understand exactly what is going on.

Investigation Is a Sober Affair: Being intoxicated in any way leads to all kinds of spiritual, physical, and legal liabilities. Save that cocktail or joint for *after* the investigation.

Respect the Spirits: This goes beyond not antagonizing the spirits. It also means helping the spirits when we can, and it means respecting them enough to not falsify their stories or any evidence they may or may not provide.

Respect the Environment: Whether you are investigating a pristine residential home or an abandoned warehouse, respect the space. Don't vandalize, trespass, break into, or leave garbage in these spaces.

Prioritize Living Humans: We certainly are here to assist the dead and the spirits on the other side. However, the physical world, homes, and life are all for the living. This means that if a deceased former resident of a home wants the current tenants to leave, you're gonna need to side with the current tenants. The former resident had their time here, and we can respectfully ask them to move on; if necessary, we can and should take measures to ensure they do so.

Know Your Limits: Learn to recognize and ask for help when you are in over your head. This includes times in which you may be faced with clients who are having mental health problems. Unless you are a licensed mental health professional, you should not be advising on treatment or giving diagnoses or explanations. Refer them to someone who is qualified.

Be Honest: Always be as honest and transparent as possible. Say, "I don't know," when you don't know. Don't exaggerate your personal experience or capabilities. Don't withhold pertinent information from clients. Be tactful, but be honest.

Be Safe: Take every measure necessary to ensure your safety and the safety of others. This means spiritual protection as well as physical protection. Be smart, travel in pairs, and let someone know where you will be. Don't ever go into a stranger's home by yourself to investigate. If you investigate in abandoned places, make sure you have an asbestos-grade mask and are up to date on your tetanus shots. Learn to recognize potential dangers, and always use your head.

The Team

This work requires organization and cooperation. If you choose to work with others, you will need to function as a team, meaning everyone will have a special role to play, but the chain of command should be clear. Every team should have a leader. This person should have both the investigative know-how and the people skills to handle the job. Having someone in charge simply makes everything go much more smoothly; everything stays organized and everyone knows their jobs. Investigations can quickly devolve into people deferring to each other endlessly into the night without someone there to call the shots. Apart from a team leader, I recommend you have a tech person, an occult person, at least one psychic, a case manager, and investigators. Let's look at each of these in detail.

Tech Manager

Your tech person is invaluable. Someone to set up, monitor, and maintain audio and visual recordings is a blessing if you are looking for evidence. This person will be in charge of changing and charging batteries—a common dilemma in this type of work—and maintaining the equipment. Your team may also choose to use fancier tech, such as infrared and FLIR thermal-imaging devices, which would fall under the jurisdiction of the tech manager as well. This person would also transport the equipment to the investigation site and distribute the devices to the investigators as necessary, such as K2 meters and digital recorders, and then collect them at the end.

Occult Specialist

If you are reading this book on paranormal witchcraft, it's a fair guess that you are going to be the team's occult person. Whether it is you or someone else, this person should have a thorough knowledge of magical practice and theory and be able to accurately identify signs of occult activity. This person may also be called on to help resolve the haunting through spells or rituals. This person should have not only knowledge, but experience.

Psychics and Mediums

The team I am on is made up mostly of psychics, and we have one of the best track records in our region for successfully resolving hauntings. In my opinion, working with psychics is imperative, and they function a little like a translator does if you were to go to a foreign country. You are there to help spirits, and if you can't see them, hear them, or feel them enough to understand them, you won't be able to do much. Your psychics should work well with others, and they should be vetted. Reach out to other groups and see whom they work with or if they have any recommendations. If you need further proof, take your potential psychic candidate to a haunted location where they have never been and ask them what they are picking up on. Be wary of any performative or overly dramatic individuals; they should fit in. All of their psychic impressions received during an investigation should be recorded and submitted to the case manager for filing.

Case Manager

A good case manager is key to this work, and they may even be more important than the team leader. They are in charge of maintaining all of the documents, evidence, and notes from the investigations. They should keep all paperwork organized by case and assign case numbers as necessary. A case manager is in charge of scheduling, communicating, and otherwise gluing the whole team together. Usually, this person is the point of contact for the team as well, and all new client emails should go to them for reviewing before being passed over to an interviewer and alerting the rest of the team. If you find a good case manager, treat them right. It's a hard job, and competent managers are hard to find.

Investigators

Last, but certainly not least, are your investigators. These are the backbone of any investigation team. They are the ones who do the evidence collecting and the exploring. All photography, K2 sweeps, and EVP sessions will be conducted by the investigators. Within the category of investigator, you may have individual jobs like an interviewer or someone who oversees speaking with the clients and doing intake meetings to document their stories. You may also want a historical researcher among your investigators, or perhaps an artist who can do sketches of spirits the clients have seen.

Some of these jobs may overlap: your occult person may also be an investigator, or your leader may be a psychic. As long as the dynamic works for your team, each person may have a couple of jobs.

Debunking

In paranormal circles, debunking has come to mean the process of ferreting out mundane causes of perceived paranormal activity. For instance, a common occurrence in hauntings is a knocking sound coming from within the walls of the home. Sounds paranormal, right? Not always. Pack rats, a common rodent in the US, are known to make this sound as well. If this is proven to be the cause, then there might not be a haunting, just a rodent problem. A debunker's main job is to eliminate other possible explanations and help you figure out what may or may not be going on in the home. They help make sure that our investigations are ethical and grounded.

That being said, outside of paranormal circles, debunking commonly means to uncover fraud. So, I recommend not announcing to your client that you are the "team debunker" or that you've brought a "debunker" along with you. This often unintentionally sends the message to your client that you are suspicious of them or that you think they are trying to trick you. This can cause a breach of trust. Instead, I recommend introducing the debunker as some-one who checks for natural and mundane problems that might be affecting the situation. A contractor, handyman, or home inspector will often make a good debunker because they are acquainted with normal home issues that may seem paranormal. Plus, they usually aren't afraid of a crawl space.

Second, require your debunker to provide proof of their asser-tions. If they are saying the disturbance is a pack rat, they should be able to show you evidence and not just provide you with a plausible explanation. Just because something *could* have been faked doesn't mean it was, and just because it *could* have a natural explanation doesn't mean it does. Proof is paramount.

The Terminology

Sometimes when you get around para folks, it can seem like they are speaking an entirely different language. To give you a head start, I'm including a list of terms you may come across and will need to understand.

EVP

EVP stands for "electronic voice phenomena" and is used to describe the process of catching disembodied voices on an elec-tronic recording device, usually a digital voice recorder. It is believed that even though we can't hear the spirits with our physi-cal ears, some devices may be able to capture the sound they pro-duce and make it available on playback. This is a common thing that most people will have seen on television, and it usually entails someone with a recording device asking questions like, "Did you die here?" or "What is your name?" The recording is then played back in hopes of finding a response to these questions.

PK

PK is short for "psychokinesis." This is a scientific term for the ability to move objects—or otherwise affect your environment—with your mind. While this may seem a little fringe, you'd be surprised at how often the term comes up and how frequently you'll see the phrase "PK activity" used throughout this book.

EMF

EMF stands for "electromagnetic field." These fields are quite common and are found in every home that is hooked up to power or plumbing. It is believed that sudden spikes in EMF may indicate spiritual activity. The trouble is that so many things give off EMF nowadays that it's hard to definitively say that a ghost is indeed producing it. Either way, some interesting experiments can be done with an EMF measuring device, which we'll discuss in a moment.

Something else to notice about EMF is the effect it has on us as humans. Many things in our home, from our breaker box to our Wi-Fi router, give off EMF. Humans who are exposed to high amounts of EMF may experience anxiety, paranoia, and hallucinations (both auditory and visual), as well as nausea and other sicknesses. This is something to consider, as high EMF in a home from some bad wiring or a poorly placed electronic device may mimic a haunting. Be sure to do preliminary EMF readings to see where it spikes and how it may be affecting the people in the home.

K2 Meter

A K2 meter is used to measure EMF. You can use this device to look for natural hot spots around the house; plumbing and electrical wiring will cause spikes in EMF. It can also be used to detect changes in EMF, which may indicate a spiritual presence. While a spike in EMF does not definitely say that a ghost is present, it can be used as a handy communication device. When placing one of these meters in a low-EMF zone, you may ask a spirit to make the K2 "jump to red" in response to a question. The K2 shows you measured EMF through colored lights: green being low, then moving up through yellow and orange to red, which signifies high EMF. You can often have very interesting conversations with spirits using a K2 and a code. For instance, "If your name is Harold, make the meter jump twice." If it does, you have your answer.

Mel Meter

This is a newer device that can be quite handy. Much like a K2, a Mel meter will measure fluctuations in EMF. However, it has the added bonus of measuring temperature at the same time. When it registers a significant fluctuation in either temperature or EMF, it will emit a sound to let you know. This means that if you leave it in the next room, it will act a bit like an assistant or another investigator. The Mel meter was designed by an electrical engineer named Gary Galka, who lost his daughter Melissa in a tragic car accident. He created the device to try to communicate with her spirit and named it after her.

ADC

ADC stands for "after-death communication." This is when someone receives a sign or miracle from someone who has passed on. These are usually small and often seem completely coincidental, such as seeing a butterfly or hearing a song on the radio. However, for the receiver of the communication, it's much more. ADC is often accompanied by an overwhelming "feeling" that most say they can't describe. They simply know that the event or sign comes from a deceased loved one.

Pareidolia

Pareidolia is a funny thing that our brains like to do and is often described as a psychological phenomenon in which our mind imposes meaningful patterns or shapes on random data or designs. Most often in paranormal work, this manifests as people seeing faces in everything. We've all looked at a cloud or a tree or some other mundane object or pattern and seen a face; it's only natural. It's best to be aware of this when going through your evidence. A lot of folks catch low-resolution anomalies in their photos and see faces and then assume it's a spirit. Always ask yourself, "Is it really a face? Or is my brain just making it into one?"

Orb

Here we've stumbled into controversial territory. Some folks are pro-orbs, while others are anti-orbs—but we'll get into that in a moment. Orbs are a type of light phenomenon that is often attributed to the presence of ghosts or spirits. You've probably seen a photo before with a floating ball of light somewhere in it. A lot of folks will say, "It's a ghost!" but honestly, it's usually just dust. What most folks don't understand is that finding orbs on film is more of a recent trend, thanks to television. Back in the day, investigators did indeed count orbs as evidence; however, they weren't necessarily orbs on film, but orbs in real time seen with the naked eye. It's not unheard of for spirits to make themselves known by appearing as balls of light that flit through a home or up ahead of you on a forest path. However, that's much harder to capture and much harder to reproduce for television, so shows often rely on film exclusively.

Now, is it always dust? No, sometimes it's a bug or a natural light anomaly. I do believe that on occasion spirits can and will appear on film as an orb, and I still feel it is something that should be considered when going over your evidence. Just make sure it seems significant. For instance, if your security camera records footage of a ball of light flying across a room, that's interesting, but not very convincing. However, if the ball of light flies across the room and into a stack of books that then fall off the shelf? Well, then you have my attention.

Spirit Box

One of the more exciting gadgets we have at our disposal is something called a spirit box or a ghost box. These are essentially little radio receivers that scan through radio frequencies very quickly. As it does this, it pumps out a lot of white noise, but occasionally a word or two will get through—mostly gibberish, but occasionally something interesting happens. Since the channels and frequencies are being flipped through so rapidly and randomly, there is little to no chance that something meaningful should come through. However, I've seen them used with surprising results. Full sentences, even paragraphs, can come through the spirit box, all made up of words and voices pulled out of the air—and usually in response to specific questions. As a psychic, I can tell you that when one of these is turned on, they draw a crowd of spirits who are curious about them. If you'd like a weird story, look up Frank's Box, the original ghost box that was designed to contact extraterrestrials.

Ovilus

An Ovilus is a bit like a spirit box but slightly more complicated. The Ovilus is a device that scans the environment and, based on the data it picks up, such as EMF, temperature changes, and so on, will produce a word. The idea is that spirits can influence the device to get messages to us.

Trigger Object

Sometimes you will hear about investigators using something they call a trigger object. This is simply an object used to trigger a response from a spirit. These can be just about anything. For instance, if the spirit the investigators are trying to contact is a child, they may put out children's toys to see if the spirit will attempt to play with them. Or if the entity seems to be demonic in nature, certain religious items will also trigger a response. Sometimes, though, trigger objects can be unkind. Some investigators will bring out things the spirit is known to fear, such as presenting certain medical devices to spirits trapped in a sanitorium where they were brutally tortured. Please keep in mind that it's always best to be kind to spirits. Not only is it the right thing to do, but working *with* the spirits will always get you better results than working *against* the spirits.

Conducting an EVP Session

One of the ways that paranormal investigators will attempt to gather evidence is through an EVP. When someone takes an audio recording in a haunted home, they'll occasionally catch an unknown voice on the tape. This is often considered to be the voice of a ghost that we were unable to hear without technical assistance. The process is simple, and the results can be quite startling.

To begin, you will want an audio recording device. Most cell phones come with a voice-recording feature; however, some folks prefer to use a separate digital voice recorder, and yet others swear by analog. They all work the same, but there is a belief that digital works best when there is some sort of steady ambient noise in the background, whether that's actual white noise played softly by another device, or something like a running faucet. Play around and you'll find what you like best. You'll want to place your recording device on something soft like a pillow or a folded towel to keep it from picking up vibrations from the ground. I do this even if I'm not placing the recorder on the floor, as the more steps you can take to reduce interference, the better. I also don't recommend holding the device while doing a session, as small adjustments from your hand may produce distortions or anomalies on the recording. I take my EVP sessions very seriously, and if I'm running point on an investigation, I will insist that everyone sit down. A couple of steps, a shifting of weight from side to side, or the rustle of a jacket can all come up as an artifact on the recording. Sitting down reduces a lot of these, and folks should remain as still as possible throughout the session.

When the recording first starts, the point person will want to state the date, time, geographical location, the names of the people who are present, and any information that would identify the exact location within the building (for example, "second-floor master bedroom" or "first-floor guest room"). You may then begin to address the haunting. Always remember that any time you begin communicating with the other side, it is very important that you specify what exactly it is that you are agreeing to interact with. So, state very clearly, "We are speaking to the spirits that haunt this house." If you just say, "Is there anything out there that wants to speak with us?" then you're going to be accidentally inviting in all kinds of things from every dark corner of the universe—and that can lead to a very bad day. Once you've specified who it is you are speaking to, you may begin to ask questions. You may ask anything you want to know, but be sure to wait five to ten seconds between each question to give the spirit time to respond. If there is an audible noise like a sneeze, a cough, or a car horn in the distance, you'll want to mark it out loud so it's on the recording. For instance, if your friend coughs, you'd simply say, "Mark it, Steven coughed," directly after. This way, when you are reviewing the audio, you won't mistake it for a ghostly artifact.

When you go to review the audio, it's best to go over it carefully while using good-quality headphones. Do so in forty-five-minute sessions and then take a break. Your ears lose their sensitivity after too long, and honestly, it can be quite tedious, so taking breaks will keep you sane.

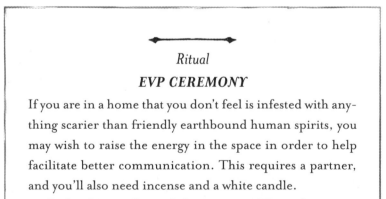

Ritual

EVP CEREMONY

If you are in a home that you don't feel is infested with anything scarier than friendly earthbound human spirits, you may wish to raise the energy in the space in order to help facilitate better communication. This requires a partner, and you'll also need incense and a white candle.

Light the candle and the incense. These things are believed to raise the energy of a space. If you wish to light more than one candle around the room, that is fine, but make sure you have at least one sitting between you and your partner. You should both ground yourselves (see page 10) and draw up the energy from the earth into your body and down your arms to your palms. See the energy forming into a ball in the palm of each hand. Carefully pass your hands over the flame of the candle, and as you do so, see the ball of energy become a beautiful golden-white light. Partner A then extends their hands out, palms up, and Partner B brings their hands to hover, palms down, over the top of Partner A's. Visualize the golden-white spheres melding together, and feel them grow to the size of grapefruits. You may rock your hands back and forth or gently circle them to feel the golden-white sphere shifting. If you are having trouble connecting, hum together for a few moments to harmonize your energies. Now, with your breath, call more energy up from the ground and pour it into the orbs, seeing them filling the room with that beautiful warm light that is available for the spirits to utilize to make EVPs and other phenomena. Continue with this until you feel like it's enough.

Conducting an Investigation

Generally, my investigations follow a standard format, beginning with first contact and ending with client homework. Every investigation will be a little different, and each team will have its own way of doing things, but the steps that I recommend are as follows: first contact, intake, investigation, resolution, and client homework.

Each of these is uniquely important, but given your style of work or group dynamic, they could be rearranged. A lot of the time, I skip the investigation portion entirely and roll it in as part of the resolution step. You'll find what works best for you, and we'll go through each in depth next.

First Contact

First contact is your first interaction with the new client. Most commonly, this is through a website or social media page. These are useful because you can utilize contact forms that capture the client's details. I'm not very tech savvy, so I usually stick with email. It's best not to give out your phone number or address information, though. This is because it's not uncommon to have folks call you in the middle of the night to tell you about the aliens in their closet. Believe me, I've had it happen on more than one occasion—which brings me to the next part.

You'll need to weed out the cases that you won't be taking. That's why I like email: it gives people a chance to explain themselves and their situation in their own words, and it gives you a buffer if you decide to turn down their case. You'll come to find that a lot of the messages you get are from folks struggling with mental illness, and I've found it's best to simply not engage in these situations. This is a very real part of our work that most folks don't realize, and it's something I feel the need to be up-front about. As investigators, we need to stick to the scope of our work. Unless you are a qualified mental health professional, please do not get involved unless necessary. If you need to provide them with resources or need to contact local professionals to intervene in a crisis, please do so, but don't get personally involved.

Other messages may come from completely stable individuals, but the activity they are describing may be out of your league or something you otherwise don't feel comfortable handling. If this is the case, please refer them to someone else, preferably in your area. You need to be very honest about your limitations so that you don't put yourself or your clients at risk. If their case seems reasonable, you may move forward with the intake process.

Intake

The intake process is when you get to know your client better and get to know the details of their case. For them, this will be like the weirdest therapy session they've ever had. For you, it's a critical time to get a feel for what it is you are dealing with. You'll be looking for specific clues in the things they say that may tell you what type of haunting it is, where it may have come from, and how you might be able to fix it. This is why I always suggest that people do an intake interview. Some teams just have folks fill out a form that describes what they are experiencing, but I find that these experiences are often hard to put into a little box on a form and that folks are more likely to leave out the small details that can be really helpful. When you get them talking over a cup of coffee, a lot comes out, especially if you have the whole family gathered at once, so I highly suggest recording the audio of the conversation to refer to later. Things that you'll want to ask or listen for include:

"When did the activity start? Did anything of note happen around then? For instance, did you bring home some new antiques or remodel part of the house?" This not only helps you gauge the duration of the haunting thus far, but can give you clues as to what caused the haunting.

"Are there children involved?" If the family is experiencing a violent haunting and there are children in the home, that case immediately jumps to the top of my priority list. Second, depending on the ages of the children, this may help you sniff out whether it's a poltergeist or some other type of haunting. For this purpose, take special note of any children between the ages of nine and fifteen, particularly girls, or anyone in the home under serious pressure either emotionally or mentally.

"Is anyone in the home dabbling in the occult or practicing magic?" It's important to know what folks are doing in the home. Folks who dabble in spiritual practices like witchcraft often either intentionally or accidentally make agreements with entities. If something has been invited in, you'll need to take extra steps to remove it. Just remember that not all promises can be broken. If your client has made some sort of formal contract through ritual or ceremony, you'll need to know the fine print before you can go anywhere near it.

Now, you're probably also thinking, "Isn't *this* a book of magic? Aren't we pro-magic here?" The answer is that we are pro-*educated* magic. I clean up a lot of messes caused by people diving headfirst into the trend of witchcraft without learning the proper foundational skills, such as grounding, protection, and cleansing. We live in an era in which magic is seen as a money-making endeavor and therefore is made to look safe and marketable. This misguided branding of the work leads to a lot of paranormal problems for unsuspecting new witches, and I see more hauntings caused by "manifesting abundance" these days than those caused by Ouija boards.

"Is anyone in the home suffering from mental illness, including anxiety and depression?" Some entities are attracted to folks who are suffering from depression and can make it worse in order to feed off the energy of sadness. Same with anxiety, which is why it's important to note. A lot of entities like to prey on vulnerable people, and those with mental illness are no exception. Those with more severe forms of mental illness may be experiencing both supernatural and psychological issues simultaneously, but that is not for you to diagnose or treat. If you are working with someone who is suffering from mental health issues, please recommend that they see a professional as well. You'll be surprised how many investigators are also psychologists or therapists. If you come across one of these, be sure to get their card. Open-minded mental health professionals are like gold.

"What is the history of the home?" A lot of times, the spirits haunting a home are the people who built it or people who have died there. In rural areas, it's not unusual to have people buried near or around a home. I've worked on more than one case in which the spirit told me they were buried on the premises.

"Does the haunting affect everyone in the home or just certain individuals?" Sometimes you'll have hauntings where everyone in the family except one will have experienced something. Other times only one person will be affected and the others won't experience a thing. If it's the latter, be sure to ask what the affected person has been up to recently.

"Have you been seeing anything unusual?" You'll also want to look for any mention of small, scurrying creatures. Most often, folks will complain about something they've been seeing out of the corner of their eye. I often hear them say, "It's like a cat darting by, but we don't have a cat." They may be describing something I call "minions" (see page 158), and that could indicate a larger problem.

"Does the haunting seem to have a personality?" Many hauntings will have a certain flair to them. Some can be quite noisy and may use sounds like knocking or screeching to get a reaction out of their victims. Others will only come out at night. Poltergeist activity tends to have a sense of humor, but so can trickster ghosts. Does the spirit have an affinity for blondes? Or single men? Do they seem to dislike religious iconography? Is the activity relegated to one portion of the house? Or do they seem to be keeping people *away* from an area in the home? All these things can give you clues to what you may be dealing with or at least point you in the direction of where you need to look next.

"Does the haunting seem erratic or routine?" You can tell a lot about a haunting by its behavior. A haunting that runs on a schedule like clockwork may be a residual haunting, whereas a haunting that changes its behavior and characters abruptly or frequently may signal that there is an open portal in the home.

"How quickly has the haunting escalated?" Most often, hauntings begin slowly and build speed over time. The rate at which this happens can be very telling. Hauntings that build speed quickly can be rather aggressive and may be actively trying to create agreements with the people involved. Mild hauntings that suddenly escalate may indicate that the spirits have been around for a while but were recently agitated by something. Hauntings that started with extreme aggression out of the blue may indicate that the affected person invited it somehow, or that it was sent to them by someone else.

When you are done with the intake interview, you may want to ask yourself a few questions about what you learned, such as, "Is there a haunting? Or is someone psychic?" This happens a lot: Folks will interpret a gaggle of spirits coming to ask them for help as a haunting. Usually, if they are psychic, this is not a new problem and is something that has happened to them frequently over the course of their lives. These folks are usually mediums but haven't realized or come to terms with it. Both children and adults seem to have this issue in equal measure. Spirits will confirm this as well and tell you if someone in the home is a psychic.

Apart from learning about the client's haunting, the intake process should also include some paperwork. You'll need consent forms for all kinds of things, depending on how you do business. You'll need one that says you're allowed to investigate the premises; this one is especially important in case someone calls the police after seeing you walking around the client's home or business with a flashlight in the middle of the night. *Do not trespass or otherwise break the law in order to do an investigation. Only investigate in areas that are public or that you have permission to access.* You'll also want a form for any occasion in which you'd want to use the client's name or identifying information in any of your advertising. You will also want a waiver that protects you from liability on the off chance you trip over your shoelace and destroy a priceless heirloom. These are boring but important.

Investigation and Resolution

This next step can be broken up into two parts or be done at once. I tend to be heavily resolution-focused, so my "investigation" portion is often just a short stretch of time when I wander around the client's house and speak to their spirits. However, you may opt to make this a big event and dedicate a whole night to doing EVP recordings, psychic walk-throughs, or more. It's up to you. Before I do this, though, I like to ask the clients two questions.

The first is, "Is there anywhere in the house where you don't want me to go?" As someone who likes to just roam around while assessing what I'm working with, it's important for me to respect people's boundaries. I usually let folks know in advance that this is something I'll want to do, and usually they are fine letting me have the run of the home. I also like to get up into people's attics and down into their basements. If the client does express that an area is off-limits, always respect that, but also make a mental note of it. It's not necessarily a red flag, but there are rare instances in which entities will exert a certain amount of influence over one or more of the residents and use this to hide their nesting ground. I've had people just "forget" that they have an entire second floor to their home because of this.

The second question you'll want to ask is, "Do you want to know what I find?" Some folks absolutely can't wait to hear what you found. Others want nothing to do with it. People have varying degrees of resiliency when it comes to paranormal matters, and while some love to hang on every detail, others will outright ask you not to talk about it at all because it scares them. Respect what your clients can handle; they don't always need to know the grisly details about who was murdered in their bathtub.

If they do want to know the details, you may follow your investigation with a "reveal," which is a sit-down with them in which you tell the client what you found and what you think is the best course of action. Some folks will demand that you resolve the haunting at all costs, as they just want to be done with it. Others will suddenly become quite fond of the ghost once they know it's just the nice old man who lived there before them and not some evil creature. In this case, they are often inclined to let the ghost stay if the ghost requests. I'm not against letting an earthbound human spirit remain if they're not causing any problems and the owner of the space agrees. However, if the ghost wants to move on, or if the activity is a danger to the family, I will insist on resolving the haunting.

Before we move on, there's one more thing we need to talk about. It's really common for paranormal investigation teams to work strictly at night. Some believe that paranormal activity is heightened in the dark or that there is more activity at certain times of day, particularly around three o'clock in the morning. While I respect each team's right to investigate as they see fit, I find night investigations to be completely unnecessary. I can assure you the ghosts and entities are there during the day as well. I've done investigations both at night and during the day and have felt no difference other than my willingness to stay awake. I recommend you try both and see which you prefer. The only situation in which I have strict rules on these things is if you are attempting an exorcism of any kind. If that is the case, do it during the day.

Client Homework

I always give clients homework to do after I leave. Usually, this includes a packet full of information covering simple things like grounding and shielding techniques, protocols for home cleansing, and any other educational materials that I feel will help them to not need me in the future. After all, the goal is to help them stand on their own. I also give them the following advice:

"Start a new cleansing routine." A lot of the time, even when a home has been successfully exorcised, the last threads or echoes of the haunting may linger, or the entity may try to come back. This is completely normal and is why you should have clients continue to do cleansings even after you leave. I usually teach them to cleanse in a way that works for them and then recommend that they do so once a day for the first week after I leave, then once a week for the next couple of months, then move out to once every two weeks, and eventually go to just once or twice a month from then on out. This not only helps to clear any lingering bits of the haunting, but it also makes the home unappealing to returning entities.

"Move on as if nothing happened." This is important to keep folks from inviting the haunting back in. The days, weeks, and sometimes months following the resolution are the most crucial. If they want to tell the story six months later, they can, but in the meantime, I suggest they don't dwell on it. It's common for exorcised entities to attempt to come back quite quickly or for a haunting to leave echoes. This is normal and may cause knocking in the home or other minor disturbances. The clients need to ignore it and move on as if it doesn't exist; it will quickly stop altogether (especially if they are following the cleansing routine). They should avoid talking about it or replaying the events in their head for several weeks. A casual thought or brief mention of it won't hurt, but the whole family reliving the events together and reigniting their fear is often enough to bring the haunting right back in. Some folks can handle speaking about it without danger because they do so without fear and with complete confidence that it is over. Not everyone can carry this energy, though.

"Throw a party." Usually, a resolution requires heavy cleansing, and therefore a lot is removed from the energy of the home and something else will need to take its place. It's best if the newly emptied home is filled with laughter and fun. I suggest folks cook dinner together, invite friends over, or watch a funny movie. I also suggest putting on their favorite uplifting music that makes them feel happy or otherwise positive. This helps set the tone for the new chapter in their life and helps them move on from the fear and struggle of their haunting. Some folks will require counseling after a haunting, and this is okay. Folks from many walks of life join the paranormal community, and you may make connections with local investigators who are also licensed therapists to whom you may be able to refer people.

Don't forget to leave them with some educational materials so they are prepared in the event of a future haunting. If you want, you can even direct them to this book, or give them a copy if it seems appropriate for them.

A Word on Obsession

While most of us can agree that the world of the paranormal is fascinating, you should be cautious. There's something called "paranormal obsession" that can happen to folks, especially when they first start out in this work. This usually looks like folks starting to do EVP or Ouija board sessions every day, or paying huge sums of money to psychics, in order to chase the rush of receiving evidence. Some folks go too far and lose touch with the outside world and their friends and families, and they eventually go a little mad and become susceptible to paranormal forces.

Whether this obsession is caused by normal means like any other addiction, or whether it's some sort of supernatural spell cast over the person by a malicious entity, we don't know. My advice is, make sure you have other interests and hobbies outside of this work, and avoid doing paranormal investigation activities every day. This advice goes double if you are still grieving the loss of a loved one.

CHAPTER 5
Understanding a Haunting

There are four main types of haunting: residual, earthbound human, poltergeist, and inhuman entity. Each type of haunting needs to be handled in a specific way. For instance, you can't attempt to fix a poltergeist in the same way you'd resolve an earthbound human haunting. They aren't the same thing and don't play by the same rules. This chapter serves to walk you through the basic landscape of a haunting and give you some foundations to build on over the course of this book. Later you'll learn the techniques associated with dealing with each of the four types of haunting, but if you don't first understand the basics, you'll have a much harder time being successful in your work. So, without further ado, let's get started, shall we?

How Does One Get Haunted?

A frequently asked question I get is, "How did this happen?" or, "What triggers a haunting?" Because let's face it: sometimes folks live in a home peacefully for over a decade, and then one day, *boom!* They're haunted. So, whether your client has bought a home that has a long history of activity or their long-time residence is suddenly acting up, here are some of the most likely culprits.

You Did Something

Most commonly, a haunting is caused by something the family has done. I can't tell you the number of times I've gone to a home and the family claims they have no idea how any of it started. It just came out of the blue! Then, about five seconds later, the spirits tell me they were invited. I then come back to the family and ask again, and that's when they begin to exchange nervous glances. Suddenly, one of them spills the beans: "Well, you see, there was this Ouija board…" or, "Well, I wanted to try witchcraft, so I got this old book…" It happens more often than you would think. While Ouija boards and witchcraft aren't inherently evil, they do pose a certain risk—especially when approached haphazardly, without much prior research or preparation.

Besides dabbling in the occult, sometimes mundane tasks can trigger a haunting. Remodeling or renovating the home is a huge trigger for hauntings, as the original owners who died forty years ago may not like their handiwork smashed to bits. People get very attached to their homes, and renovations can be extremely offensive. Other times, spirits don't want their secrets coming to the surface. Maybe they hid something in a wall that they don't want found or they buried something—or someone—in the backyard, where you're digging your new pool. Construction and renovation can also open portals unwittingly.

Did You Know You're Psychic?

The second-most common reason folks are haunted is because they are psychic and don't realize it. However, the spirits do, and they are trying to make contact. When someone is a medium, spirits flock to them because they have a light. The spirits sense it and come to the person to get help. It's really common for me to be in a house where either a parent or child (or both) are chronically haunted. When I speak to the spirits, they tell me that they came because they heard that this person could help them. On speaking further with the client, it usually comes to light that they have had many paranormal experiences during their lifetime, and usually once they acknowledge and accept their gifts, they begin to have a much easier time. When you come across these folks, please always give them book recommendations or at least some basic information on navigating their psychic journey after you leave.

Location, Location, Location!

Many hauntings are simply a matter of living in the wrong place at the wrong time. Any number of things, including traumatic events (suicide, murder, rape, and deadly accidents, to name a few), can leave a serious mark on a place. This mark is like a stain, and even with deep cleaning, some stains just don't lift out and will forever loom beneath the surface of a home or piece of land. More often than not, the source of the haunting is the land, not the house itself. This is why you will sometimes find strange old spirits haunting new construction. They still remember their home being where your client's now sits. Or maybe they lived nearby and have wandered over into the home. Yes, that does happen!

A lot of folks assume that for a home to be haunted, the haunting had to originate from inside that home. However, folks are frequently haunted by spirits that died next door, or even a mile down the road. The spirit simply wandered over and liked their home for any number of reasons, such as they liked the decorating scheme or liked the children living there because they reminded them of their own. This is another unfortunate part of locational hauntings: simply being near something or someone that is haunted may inadvertently affect your client and their family.

Other locational issues are things like the local geology. Certain pieces of land carry certain minerals that are better at recording and conducting energy than others, and the deposits under or around the home may increase the risk of hauntings. Also, running water, particularly water moving underground beneath the home, can add to the risk of hauntings. These bodies of water are believed to cause swiftly moving energy currents and can occasionally become "highways" for spirits, and the home may become an accidental rest stop. Similarly, some folks say that homes that are near churches are more susceptible to demonic activity, and they often cite an old saying: "The devil will play in the shadow of a church."

Alternatively, some very famous haunted buildings are often thought to be built on some sort of portal or nexus of strange supernatural energy. These locations include places like the Cecil Hotel in Los Angeles, which is chock-full of strange and unexplainable energies. It can be nearly impossible to resolve a haunting in a place like this. Some jobs are just too big, and I have a feeling that these naturally strange places are important to the paranormal ecology of our world.

Lastly, I don't give much credence to something being an "Indian burial ground" or "Indian land" as a source of the haunting. First of all, folks should say "Native American" or "First Nations people." Second, the entire North American continent is former Native American land, including sacred land and burial ground. Unless the spirits haunting a place are indigenous people or the home is on a specific sacred location, an important burial ground, or the site of a major massacre, it's probably something else.

You Simply Stepped in It

Truly, sometimes people are just in the wrong place at the wrong time. Whether it's human spirits or malevolent entities, sometimes the client will just come across it accidentally while going about their day and something will follow them home. They open the wrong closet in the basement at work, or they bring home the wrong antique. Whatever it is, it happens. So, after a haunting begins, part of the checklist you should go through is unusual places your client has been or things they've purchased, particularly antiques or pre-owned items.

The Entity Was Sent to You

This is the least common cause of a haunting. Most spirits require agreements, particularly malevolent or inhuman entities. Therefore, most hauntings start slowly and rev up over a matter of days, weeks, months, or even years. However, if a haunting starts at a high level of activity, particularly when it comes to physical contact with the client, it's a sign that the entity may have been sent. So, if a spirit just out of the blue attacks your client without any prior haunting activity, you need to ask if the client has done anything to make an agreement with an entity. If they say they have not—and you have reason to believe they are telling the truth—you'll want to ask about any enemies they may have who are involved in occult practices. Someone can create agreements and give an entity permission to go after someone, bypassing the agreement-making process with the client (see page 161).

The Ouija Board Conundrum

I get asked all the time, "Are Ouija boards dangerous?" and the answer is both yes and no. They are not dangerous when they are just sitting there or when they are being used *correctly*. The trouble is that most folks *think* they know the proper way to use one, and many of them are gravely mistaken. Many people will loudly proclaim that a Ouija board is no different from a pendulum, a deck of tarot cards, or an EVP session. While these things are clearly not the same, what these folks fail to see is that the culture and method of use when it comes to such boards is what sets them apart from something like a pendulum, tarot cards, or an EVP device. These items can indeed be just as dangerous, but the factors surrounding the common use of Ouija boards creates a perfect storm of mistakes that can lead to all kinds of paranormal issues. These factors are often not found in other forms of divination like pendulums and tarot cards.

To begin, you must consider the common, everyday people using Ouija boards and the culture created by the lore and legend surrounding the game. If we set aside professional spiritualists and educated practitioners for a moment, the folks most commonly using Ouija boards are people at parties, including people who have been drinking or using drugs, teenagers ready to cop an attitude and challenge a wayward entity, scared people, and people who don't know how to protect themselves from spirits. All of this has an effect on which energies are attracted and the risk associated with this type of spirit contact. The fact that this is specifically a multiperson game has an effect as well—you're not supposed to play alone, according to Ouija lore—and more people means more energy to draw from and attract spirits. Furthermore, this game often involves people who are afraid, whether it's the terrified girl who was at the wrong slumber party on the wrong night, or just a group of friends on Halloween trying to spook each other. This energy attracts things that feed on fear, like chumming the water, and those things that come sniffing around are usually not friendly. Not to mention the almost built-in expectation that something scary will happen, which sets up a doorway just asking to be opened.

You then have to consider the method of use. What is the first thing folks tend to say when opening a Ouija board session? "Is there *anyone out there* who would like to communicate with us?" That's a *really* wide invitation. I've also seen people dramatically call to "the spirits," which is even more vague. This type of opening is an invitation and an agreement (see page 161) to interact and communicate with them—also known as a huge foot in the door. And what happens next? They ask the spirit to move the planchette, or pointer. Most people believe that Ouija boards work one of two ways: (1) the spirit moves the planchette, or (2) the spirit affects or influences the participants in a way that causes them to move the planchette. If their belief is the first, then they've picked the lesser of two evils and made an agreement that the spirit can manipulate objects in the room. If they believe that option number two is how it works, they've made an agreement that the spirit can perform a partial possession on them or exert influence over their physical bodies. See how this gets tricky?

Something like an EVP session is often conducted by sober, professional, adult individuals with a firm goal in mind and little to no fear. They also tend to have rather specific spirits they are trying to contact and also have some knowledge of protecting themselves. Similarly, pendulums are often used as a way to connect with your "inner knowing" or "higher self" and are used in a solitary fashion. I have no doubt that an EVP or pendulum session approached in the manner that most folks approach a Ouija board session would indeed produce concerning activity—and they occasionally do, just with much less frequency. If, however, you use a Ouija board calmly, with protections in place, set a clear intention, and are mindful of your phrasing, you should be fine. Just remember to cleanse the room before and after, say a prayer, and always, *always* say goodbye.

The Multiple-Haunting Scenario

It's not uncommon to have more than one type of haunting occurring in the same space simultaneously. This can make diagnosing the issue a little tricky. For instance, the erratic nature of a poltergeist can disguise the arrival of an inhuman entity, or a poltergeist paired with a residual haunting can look like a haunting caused by earthbound human spirits. Therefore, you should take a well-rounded look at the problem and perhaps perform a few tests to see how the haunting responds. For instance, does it seem to follow a specific person? That may indicate a poltergeist, if it fits the criteria. Does it respond in a hostile manner if you place religious objects out and about? If you try to communicate with it, does it respond? If it doesn't, it could be a residual haunting. I've also encountered human spirits with so many attachments that I have mistaken them for inhuman entities.

Diagnosing the problem can be quite difficult, so feel free to take your time and keep an open mind to all possibilities. It's rare that we'll ever know for certain what exactly is in a home, especially when we are dealing with inhuman entities, because we often don't have names or accurate vocabulary for them. Still, it's important to at least figure out which type(s) of haunting you are facing to make sure you approach a situation in the right way. If you don't correctly identify the type of haunting, it will be obvious, as the haunting will not respond to the recommended treatments. If this is the case, you may have to consider that you've misidentified the haunting or that there is a separate haunting happening concurrently.

The last thing you need to remember is that not all of the layers of a haunting are supernatural. While you may have multiple hauntings happening simultaneously, it's also common to have psychological and paranormal issues happening at once. I think that on occasion mental illness can act as an unexpected doorway to the other side. Just because your client is exhibiting signs of mental illness doesn't mean their reports of activity or spirit communication are false. Similarly, just because they are experiencing activity doesn't mean they don't also need psychological help if they are exhibiting signs of mental illness. Both of these things can be happening to them, but the psychological part needs to be handled by a trained professional.

Can You Create a Haunting from Nothing?

Yes. Surprised? Well, it's true, and it happens more often than you would think. Normally, a haunting needs to come from a source, such as a traumatic event or a spirit. However, hauntings have been known to be created by groups of normal, everyday people through the power of belief and words. In most cases, how it begins is with a story. Someone makes up a tale, maybe about "old man Richard" who used to work at the saloon and "still haunts it to this very day." The story spreads, people begin to believe it, and before long the staff at the saloon begin to experience activity. The question is, how does this happen? The answer to that question is … well, we don't know. There are a few theories, though.

The most popular explanation is that the activity is caused by a family of created spirits that includes thoughtforms, tulpas, and egregores. These are beings that are born from the power of individual or collective belief. If enough folks believe, they are subconsciously sending energy to the same place, and eventually that energy adds up to a real spirit capable of all kinds of things. This means that even though "old man Richard" never existed, his spirit may be seen in the old saloon and he will behave in accordance with the legend. For instance, he'll walk with a limp and will only be seen at happy hour if that's what's dictated by the story.

While this is the usual explanation, we must remember that paranormal riddles don't always have just one answer. We must also consider the fact that some spirits also have identity issues, and you'll come across some who don't seem to remember who they are, for one reason or another. Sometimes these spirits will assume a new identity in order to feel complete. Other times, a negative entity may assume the identity of a rumored spirit in order to gain access to certain spaces or people. All of these explanations are possible, and it's your job to sniff out which is happening.

What's Feng Shui Got to Do with It?

Have you ever rearranged your furniture and absolutely hated it? Maybe even without a real reason besides that it made the room feel "closed off" or "not welcoming" or even "suffocating"? Whether you choose to believe in the Chinese art of feng shui or not, you'll soon realize the way our environments are structured can greatly affect the flow of energy through our home. I personally am a big believer in this practice and have seen firsthand how some simple tidying or rearranging can affect a haunting. The energy in a home needs to flow smoothly, slowly, and continuously for optimum health and happiness in the home. If it moves too quickly, the energy can become harsh and cause problems with luck and health. However, if the energy becomes blocked, it will stagnate, and I've found this to be a major cause of hauntings. This stagnant energy will gum up and become the perfect nesting ground for negative entities and will attract other creatures. Nasty spirits and harmful energies will hide in clutter and mess and evade exorcism at all costs. This is why it's best to clean and declutter *before* spiritual cleansing.

A conversation you'll have to have frequently with clients is about tidiness. I've found that most homes that have major haunting issues are quite messy. If I'm unable to get to a haunted home for several days, I will often encourage the family to clean and organize their home in the meantime. Not only does this give them a much needed sense of control, but it makes my job a lot easier when I get there. In fact, you'd be surprised how much of a shift will happen in a haunting after simply cleaning, organizing, and decluttering. This helps the energy begin to flow again, making the space less suitable for hauntings.

Similarly, a handful of homes that you work on will have chronic haunting problems due to the layout of the home. Western architecture and home design does not take into account feng shui principles and can often produce homes and offices that do not allow for proper energy circulation. Some of these issues can be remedied with "cures," often in the form of rearranged furniture and carefully placed potted plants, lights, wind chimes, or mobiles. However, I've seen some homes that even tried-and-true feng shui cures can't help much, due to poor architectural design. At that point, there is not much that can be done, though I do still recommend frequent airing of the home by opening the doors and windows.

Whether you believe in feng shui as a practice or not, I highly recommend getting a feel for its basic principles, as they do come in handy when dealing with haunted homes. Depending on your location, you may even have someone who does this work professionally in your area who may agree to consult on such matters when you have a case.

Should the Family Leave the Home?

You'll find that many families are faced with the decision to either stay and fight with the haunting or abandon their home and move out. While this subject is tricky and every case is unique, in my experience it is always best that the family stay in the home unless they absolutely have to vacate for safety reasons. This is because when you abandon the home, you are forming an agreement (see page 161) with the entity that it now owns the home. You've signed over the spiritual deed, and that makes getting it back much harder. So, unless the family is ready to leave and never return, it's best that they try to stick it out as long as possible.

God, Religion, and the Supernatural

While I would like to tell you that this work is completely secular, religion and the supernatural are never quite separate. I myself identify as "Folk Catholic," meaning I believe in Jesus but also a whole mess of other stuff and practice a great deal of folk magic. My personal path will of course color much of the material in this book, and later you may see terms like *prayer* or *psalm* and references to religious figures like archangels. Why? Well, because they really do help and have made my work successful for years. I'm not asking you to become Christian; I'm simply asking you to keep an open mind when it comes to which forces you choose to ally yourself with in this work. Each technique and recipe herein is adaptable to your chosen path, and I encourage tinkering with the work.

Later in this book, we will talk about removing negative entities by cleansing and entrusting the space to a "higher power." This can be a deity that you work with, but please think it through first and ask yourself, "Is this deity a good fit for this situation?" You will have to consider the client as well. Not only would it be a potentially bad idea to give someone's guest bedroom to a wrathful goddess of death, but the client may not be comfortable with it either, or it could cause further spiritual issues in the home after you leave. Therefore, I recommend getting comfortable with the inexhaustible source of compassion, creation, justice, and love that exists in the cosmos. You don't have to call it "God" if that makes you feel weird. It can be "Goddess" or "Spirit" or whatever you need it to be. And you don't have to abandon your beliefs in favor of "love and light" rhetoric either, but it's extremely helpful to form this connection with the Divine. Just make friends with the thing up there that is loving and has humankind's best interests at heart, someone you can hand over darkness to and get light in return. If you struggle with that, you may refer to the list of helpful spirits I've made on page 151.

Now that we've discussed the basic mechanics of a haunting, in the following four chapters we'll go into the four main types: residual, earthbound human, poltergeist, and inhuman entity. Each of these hauntings are quite different from one another, and each will need to be handled in their own unique way.

CHAPTER 6
The Residual Haunting

Y ou have undoubtedly heard a ghost story about a young
woman whose husband went off to war or out to sea and never
returned. The tale usually goes that every day the poor widow would
walk to some window on the top floor of her home and look out,
hoping to see that her beloved had finally returned. She would do
this every single day for years and years until the day she died. These
stories often end with, "It's said that her spirit can still be heard walking up the stairs (or be seen from the window) to this day." But why
are these stories so common? Probably because these types of hauntings are so common. This is what we call a residual haunting.

Most folks think all hauntings are caused by a ghost or spirit
entity. However, this type of haunting is caused by memories or
echoes that get caught in the space. A residual haunting is created
when there is some sort of event that is either repeated so many
times that it becomes enmeshed in the energy of the space, or
when there is an event so powerful or traumatic that it makes an
energetic imprint on the location. This causes the home or space
to repeatedly reenact that event on a loop. The apparitions seen
are not conscious spirits but are more like a movie being projected over and over. How this happens is up for much debate (like
a lot of these phenomena), but there are two main theories that
people tend to work with when explaining the mechanics of a
residual haunting.

The first way of looking at a residual haunting requires a little background. It is understood that all things pick up energy to varying degrees. Things that are soft like fabric pick up energy easily but also release it very quickly. Harder objects like metal don't pick up energy as easily, but they also retain it much better once they do. The materials that make up your home are also capable of picking up these energies and storing them. Over time, these memories are released. It's also believed that the minerals surrounding your home will greatly impact the probability of a residual haunting. The ever-popular "stone tape theory," which says that energetic memory can be stored in rock and replayed just like a tape recording, is often cited as an explanation for this. These minerals, particularly quartz deposits, are said to provide an ideal environment for this type of haunting.

The second way folks explain the activity is the time loop theory. The idea here is that either the repeated action or the traumatic event impacts the environment to such a degree that it causes a kink to form in that moment in time. Thus, that bit of time keeps replaying over and over again until it's rebalanced. This continuous replay of events cycles in the space beside our timeline and can be felt in our world—a little like how an unbalanced washing machine can still be felt and heard from the next room. Similarly, if we think of time as being folded up like an accordion, the events may be so loud or powerful that they can be experienced in other layers of time.

Though this is one of the more enigmatic types of haunting, I believe that both explanations are correct in their own way. You'll quickly come to learn that when the paranormal is faced with a "this or that" question, the answer is usually "both." The truth is usually somewhere in the middle, or a combination of the two. In both cases, an event becomes imprinted or locked into a space in which it gets repeated. The goal is then to heal or release this event.

Identifying the Residual Haunting

Residual hauntings are different from the other three main types of hauntings in one very distinct way: the haunting does not have its own consciousness. It is simply a recording that gets played over and over again. This means that these hauntings are often easily identified by a consistency and regularity not found in the others. When first interviewing the client, watch for statements about the haunting like, "Every night at 4 a.m. the woman walks down our hallway. She never speaks and doesn't seem to see us." Very spooky, but there are several telltale signs here.

First, residual hauntings run on a loop, so they keep a schedule. They will often happen at the same time of day or otherwise keep to a routine. They also will repeat the same actions, sounds, apparitions, and so on. The second thing to notice is that the spirit does not interact with or respond to the living. It's like the people Scrooge sees in *A Christmas Carol*, when the first ghost takes him to the past. They can neither see nor hear you. They are in the past; we are just experiencing that moment in our time. Furthermore, conscious earthbound human spirits will normally respond to or interact with the living. They experience us rather clearly. On occasion, earthbound spirits will be caught in a memory or delusion, but they won't keep quite the same schedule, and they can be roused from the memory when met with cleansing smoke. For instance, the woman from the story above may continue to routinely look for her lost love even in death—she may also not even be aware she is dead—but she'll still be able to respond to an EVP session or other attempts at contact, because she is a conscious spirit. Memories can't respond.

When identifying this type of haunting, you'll want to make sure to note the consistency of the haunting as well as the schedule it runs on. Furthermore, you'll want to see if it is responsive, either by trying to talk to it or by using trigger objects. Researching the history of the home will also give you insight into potential causes of the haunting. Often library and records research will tell you the big things, but be sure to speak to neighbors and former owners of the home who may remember events or have heard stories that are not necessarily written down in the records. You'll want to look for things like tragic accidents and deaths, routine meetings and events, assaults and murders, and historical events such as battles. In places like Gettysburg, it's common for folks to see soldiers or hear cannons and gunfire. The repeating of the battle is a residual haunting caught in that space.

Addressing the Residual Haunting

When it comes to fixing or clearing up a residual haunting, we can go about it in a few ways. The trick is to understand the function of what you have to do and then choose your method accordingly. For a residual haunting, the idea is that you have to release trapped memory or vibrations in order to rebalance and restore the natural energy of the place.

Personally, I like to address this with smoke, sound, and prayer. The airy nature of these helps to lift and release the trapped energy. And while you may want to reach for fancier stuff like copal to help unblock the energy, in most cases simple incense is usually enough to get the job done. The idea is to use your will and intention to amplify the lightness of the smoke and lift away trapped vibrations. I do this through a steady stream of prayer, asking that the energies be unbound from the space and released. I ask that they become like dandelion seeds that just get carried away on the smoke of the incense. After a while, the space will take on a lightness. I also am sure to pray for the healing of the space. If you are not comfortable with prayer, you may use incantations or read appropriate excerpts of poetry, and you can play uplifting music, especially classical music, to take the place of the words as well. Apart from smoke, sound may also be used to treat the issue. Things like singing bowls, resonant bells, and tuning forks may be used to lift and harmonize stuck energy.

Sometimes the memory can be healed as well. Those with training in energy healing modalities like Reiki may send healing to the space and affect great change. A residual haunting can be viewed as a location with unhealed trauma, and even though a room or a house is not a person, that does not mean it doesn't need healing. Similarly, changing the feng shui in a home can unblock the trapped energy. I encourage you to try all of these and to combine them in different ways to see what you like best.

Unfortunately, even given our best efforts, a residual haunting can be like a stain. You can scrub it and treat it in all kinds of ways, but at the end of the day, some stains lift right out while others are permanent and can never be fully removed. Some residual hauntings will be the same way and, depending on how they were created, might not be fixable. If you find that your normal spiritual methods are not working on a particular case, the clients can attempt to fix it through home improvement. Sometimes a simple remodel, a fresh coat of paint, and a deep cleaning will do more than incense and bells. Even then, you may be stuck with the haunting. The good news is that residual hauntings are not dangerous and often pose little more than an inconvenience to those living in the home.

CHAPTER 7
Earthbound Human Spirits

The classic haunting is, of course, caused by a ghost—a deceased human with some sort of unfinished business. While this is only one-fourth of the possible haunting scenarios, earthbound human spirits are ubiquitous in this work, and even when they aren't necessarily the problem, they'll be found in most of the homes you will visit. This means that understanding their world and how they function is imperative to this work.

When we die, our spirit is supposed to make its way through "the light," or the doorway to the next place. However, a good number of folks don't end up making this very important transition and choose to remain here in our earthly plain, either of their own free will or because they are trapped here for one reason or another. This is why we call these spirits "earthbound." Human spirits that remain earthbound for any reason will all function in the same way and be subject to the same problems. However, it's not all bad: some of them greatly enjoy their afterlife in our plane of existence, and some even take up a job or otherwise form community with other souls like them. The best example of this I can think of is the day I met a ghost named Ruthe.

I was hanging out in an old, dusty bar with the lovely ladies of Hela Paranormal, an investigative group out of the Portland metro area, when they told me that they had been invited to investigate the ever-elusive Montgomery House in Kalama, Washington, and they wanted me to go with. I had heard the name before and knew it was a famously haunted location, but I knew absolutely nothing about it—which, honestly, I prefer. They said the house had new owners who hadn't been allowing any investigations until now, and we would be given first shot at it. I was ecstatic and eagerly accepted their offer.

On December 28, 2019, we arrived at the home and found ourselves standing out front, clutching our gear in the murky light of dusk. Even from the sidewalk looking up at the house, it seemed ominous, and I could hear a faint whispering coming from inside that let me know the rumors were indeed true. It was stuffed to the gills with spirits. Once we got inside, the group began chatting with the homeowners, but I was distracted by something else. At the top of the stairs in front of me was the spirit of an older woman, probably in her mid-fifties, with an early 1900s style of dress and a stern face. Her energy was severe, and I could tell immediately that she was in charge and this was *her* home. As I stood staring, I realized I was not the only one; my friend Zee from Hela Paranormal was standing beside me, looking up at the top of the stairs and scribbling wildly on her phone using a stylus and a drawing app. Even though I hadn't spoken a word, I looked down and realized she was drawing the exact woman I was seeing.

Through our investigation at Montgomery House, we got to know Ruthe quite well. We confirmed she was a former owner of the home and had run it as a boardinghouse in the early twentieth century. In fact, she still was running the home as a boardinghouse, except now her home was open to the dead instead of the living. I followed her around the home as she went from room to room, straightening things and checking on her guests. She was very aware that she was dead and showed no signs of the wear and tear of being earthbound for so long. No doubt, her intense focus and sense of purpose aided her in remaining quite lucid. She had several permanent guests in the home, but Ruthe let me know in no uncertain terms that she kept them all in line. She ruled the house with an iron fist, and even when we found a strange entity in the basement, it was clear that it stayed down there because it was afraid of her.

To this day, Ruthe is still managing the boardinghouse for wayward ghosts who need a place to stay. She runs a tight ship and demands that her guests behave. Without her, I shudder to think what the house would be like. Montgomery House is a residential home now and is considered private property.

Why Are They Earthbound?

To understand and work with earthbound spirits, you first have to understand how they came to be earthbound in the first place. Each spirit will have their own unique reason for not crossing over, and discovering this reason is helpful when counseling the spirit and resolving the haunting. I've come to understand that there are some common reasons you are likely to see over and over again.

Unfinished Business

We've all heard this one before. Some spirits will refuse to move on because there was something important they didn't get to do before they died. This can be just about anything, ranging from not being able to tell a loved one goodbye to needing to finish a last will and testament. These things can be extremely important to some folks and therefore become anchors for spirits that hold them back from crossing over. Same thing with secrets they feel they need to protect and make sure no one stumbles across, like buried sums of money or a letter in a chest detailing a lurid affair.

They Are Afraid

A surprising amount of the time, the reason a spirit chooses to remain earthbound is because they are afraid of the light or what lies beyond it. This is especially common when the person did not lead an exemplary life and the spirit fears that by passing into the light they will be taken to hell or otherwise punished for the things they have done. People who took their own life are also likely to be afraid of the light for the same reason. However, in my experience of speaking with spirits who have committed suicide, there is no punishment waiting on the other side for them.

The earthbound spirits of children are often held back by fear as well. They are often frightened and confused and find themselves hiding from the light because they don't know what it means. Many times, the spirits of children will become earthbound because they are waiting for their parents to go with them, help them through, or otherwise let them know that it's okay.

They Don't Know They Are Dead

It's common for spirits to not know they are dead. This happens most often when they died suddenly, such as being hit by a bus. As the body is ripped away, the spirit may simply keep walking and going about their life. Also, on occasion, this can be a result of the spirit being unable to cope with being dead, and therefore they simply refuse the idea and continue on as normal. When this happens, they can rationalize a great deal and remain "alive" in their own mind for quite a long time. Think Bruce Willis in *The Sixth Sense*.

Waiting for or Watching Over Family

Many spirits choose to remain earthbound so they can watch over loved ones and family members. Whether it's their children or spouses, many will try to protect and guide them from the other side. What many of these spirits don't realize is that they can indeed come back after passing through the light. In fact, it's better for them to go through the light and come back than it is to remain earthbound, as this makes them stronger and less susceptible to astral predators and parasites. A great number of spirits will also try to wait for family members to pass through the light with them, but this is also unnecessary.

They're Having Too Much Fun

Ever wondered if there is a ghost watching you in the shower? Truth is, there probably is. People who were mischievous or voyeuristic in life will continue to be so in death. This includes not only trickster folk, but criminals and other unsavory people as well. Many folks choose to remain earthbound because they are having a blast without a body. They can spy, go through walls, and do whatever they want without consequences. This is a mischievous person's dream!

They're Trapped

Many spirits will suffer from some form of trauma, usually related to events that happened in their lives that they've brought with them into the spirit dimension. This will manifest for them in several ways: they will either be trapped in the physical place where they felt trapped in life, or they will continue to relive their trauma over and over again like the most messed-up version of *Groundhog Day*. To give a couple of examples, one of the first spirits I helped cross over was trapped in my aunt's basement. The ghost of a young girl haunted this basement because her abusive father used to lock her down there, and it became her prison in death. I've also come across ghosts who were stuck at work 24-7, unable to leave because it was their life, and it then became their afterlife.

Others relive their death over and over again. As always, each case is unique. These spirits are often mistaken for residual hauntings, but you'll notice they aren't quite as consistent.

Sometimes these spirits will respond when spoken to, in which case you can sort of talk them out of the endless cycle and bring them back to clarity. Once you explain what is going on, they'll often come back to their senses rather quickly. Most spirits in this situation don't know they are dead. Others will be too far gone to respond at first, but hitting them with some cleansing smoke will often bring them back to their senses, at which point you can speak to them.

The Living Won't Let Them Go

Some folks will be surprised to find that the living have a lot of sway over their dead loved ones, especially during the time shortly after their passing. It's not uncommon to find that the reason some spirits can't move on is because the living won't let them go. This only happens in extreme cases in which the living are overcome by grief and actively wish and hope so desperately to have their loved ones near that it creates an energetic leash that keeps the spirit from being able to cross over through the light. Only by counseling the family to accept the death and let the person go will their spirit be allowed to cross.

In other rare circumstances, a spirit may be held back because the family is only remembering the person near the time of their death. For example, if you are only remembering your deceased parent as old, sick, frail, and hooked up to all kinds of tubes and monitors in the hospital, then you may be inadvertently keeping them trapped in that state and unable to move on. Therefore, it's important to remember the good times and remember them when they were vibrant and healthy. *Please remember that this is quite rare;*

a thought or memory of their last days won't have an impact on them, but dwelling constantly on *only* these memories may have an adverse effect.

Problems with Remaining Earthbound

While many human spirits choose to remain earthbound, it can be risky. To remain in the in-between space is unnatural and goes against the "natural order of things." This natural order is to die and then move on through the light to the next place. The space between is meant to be little more than a layover, or a brief moment to say goodbye before moving on. Staying in that transitional space is a bit like a baby deciding to stay in the birth canal indefinitely. Still, the spirit world, like nature, has its own way of dealing with those who remain behind. Let's discuss why this happens, and what happens when it does.

They Need Living Human Energy

Earthbound spirits cannot sustain themselves without a body like many other types of spirits can. They need to absorb living human energy to function in this form.[1] This is why you can often find earthbound spirits in places where the living congregate. Shopping malls, movie theaters, bars, and so on are all paranormal hot spots because they produce a lot of human energy. To earthbounds, our energy works a bit like joint lube or a strong cup of coffee. It simply helps them function. Without it, they will grow slow and lethargic before they simply fade away. It takes a lot of time to do so, but it will happen eventually.

---

1. Mary Ann Winkowski, *When Ghosts Speak: Understanding the World of Earthbound Spirits* (New York: Grand Central Publishing, 2007), 42.

This also explains quite a bit of haunting activity. You see, many earthbounds will cause disruption in order to create fright or frustration in living people. When we have a reaction to something, we throw off energy, and that is something they can feed on. For instance, you've probably seen or heard of batteries draining quickly from devices like flashlights and cameras during paranormal investigations. A lot of folks will tell you the spirits are draining the battery as a means of gathering energy. However, what is probably happening is the spirits are messing with the batteries to get an excited, frustrated, or fearful response from the living, which gives them usable energy. It's not the batteries that feed them; it is your reaction to the disturbance.

Predators and Parasites

Much like nature, the spirit world is full of predators, scavengers, and parasites. Most folks think that the spirit world is simply dead humans and animals, but the truth is there is a vast number of unearthly creatures living there that are looking to either feed on or collect earthbound spirits caught in the space between. The most common type we find are parasites. These attach to spirits like barnacles and feed off their energy until the spirits are completely dissolved. However, much like leeches and other parasitic creatures, one is generally not enough to do the job on its own. Over time, earthbound spirits will often pick up multiple parasites. I've even come across spirits that are so covered in them that I've mistaken the spirits for inhuman entities. When a spirit falls victim to parasites, they often become agitated, lethargic, and irritable. These ghostly barnacles drain their energy and sometimes cause them to become aggressive.

Apart from parasites, there is a whole world full of inhuman entities that also prey on earthbound spirits. It's hard to list them all individually, because there are so many different kinds and most of them have not been catalogued with names or labels. Some of them hunt and eat earthbound spirits. Others collect earthbound spirits, which is the most unnerving thing I've ever come across. Some even make displays out of them, like a strange museum of trapped souls. I've also seen religious cults made up of earthbound spirits all following an inhuman leader disguised as a preacher. I don't know what the overall purpose of such collections are, but the spirit world is strange that way.

While these creatures aren't very common, they're the main reason why I tell earthbound spirits to go through the light and come back if they are planning on protecting or watching over a loved one. If they remain earthbound, they are at risk and more likely to end up a snack than a protector. After going through the light, they will be much stronger and much less vulnerable to spiritual predators.

The Madness, and Then the Change

People usually think that most ghosts come from times we have romanticized and were pioneers, people from the Renaissance, Vikings, or other ancient people. However, once you begin doing paranormal investigation, you'll realize that really old earthbound human spirits are quite rare. Most are from the last three hundred years or less. This is because human spirits are not meant to remain earthbound. Many human spirits who stay here too long eventually develop a sickness. It starts as an irritability, or a sadness, and becomes hostility and confusion. Over time, this sickness develops into full-blown madness. As the sickness progresses, the earthbound spirit will begin to change, and they will either become violent or breathtakingly sad, each day becoming less and less human. After *many* years, the spirit devolves into a strange, inhuman entity.

Many things affect this process, but overall, this slow degradation over many decades seems inevitable. We simply aren't meant to remain here after death. All things decay on this side of the light.

Some spirits devolve into the sickness faster than others, depending on certain factors. In my experience, those who are at peace in the in-between, such as a warm-hearted old man who simply wants to remain in the house he built, and who doesn't cause much trouble besides the occasional whiff of cigar smoke, may stay behind for quite some time before the sickness even begins to set in. On the other hand, restless, angry, lost, or confused spirits will succumb to the process faster. Many of the accelerating and inhibiting factors associated with this phenomenon are based on the personal constitution of the spirit, but there are several other things that seem to either speed up or slow down the process. The presence of spirit parasites speeds up the sickness, as does a lack of living human contact. However, having a job or a purpose seems to slow down the process, as does hanging around the living—like Ruthe, still running the boardinghouse: this sense of purpose and focus kept her not only strong, but free of the madness. She was a formidable spirit and had living tenants who own the home to keep her fed.

But what is it that these spirits change into? It's hard to say, and possibly even harder to describe. I'm not sure I'd call them negative entities, but they transform into something… *different*. Something strange and occasionally hostile. They are the shadowy husks of human spirits completely stripped of their humanity. They are often lumpy and twisted and eventually become unrecognizable, inhuman spirits. As if it can't get any weirder, the presence of elementals—sprites, gnomes, nymphs, and so on—may also affect the transformation. I have come across a case in which a human spirit was halfway through the change in a home with a natural spring in the basement. The spring was inhabited by tricky water elementals that took a liking to this strange, Quasimodo-esque, half-human, half-something else creature. They decided to adopt it, and not only that, they decided to turn it into one of them. This was one of the oddest things I've ever encountered, and I've seen some weird stuff. Over time, they had sort of decorated it with aquatic plant spirits, and it had physically begun to resemble them, only much larger and, well, weirder. The sight was chilling.

Counseling Earthbound Human Spirits

We must remember that all earthbound human spirits or "ghosts" are people—more specifically, people who are going through the strangest, most confusing experience of their lives. This means that they may need a little help or someone to talk to. Most dead folks didn't get a supernatural education during their lifetimes, and honestly, nothing on the other side resembles anything you'll hear about in church on Sunday. Having someone to explain what is happening to them is not only comforting but extremely helpful. Sometimes just getting some clarity on their situation is enough to get them to move on on their own. Even just having the epiphany that they are dead will sometimes open the light. More often than not, the light is already open and near them, but they can't see it through their own cloudy perception.

When we speak to earthbound spirits, it's always best to do so from a place of compassion. You are often delivering news that is hard to hear. Being patient and understanding is the best approach. Some spirits need to spend a little more time digesting the information than others. Others may refuse to go through the light at all and choose to remain earthbound. Either way, by using the information in this book, you can better explain what is happening to them and what they can expect, depending on which path they choose. Remember, the spirits of children and those with cognitive disabilities may need a gentler touch than others.

Exercise

OPENING THE LIGHT

One of the most important and fulfilling techniques you can learn in this work is to open the light. That's right, *you* can open the light and help spirits cross over into the next realm. You don't need any fancy tools, just your mind and a willing spirit. It's deceptively simple, but incredibly satisfying, to be able to help a spirit who has been trapped for so long to cross over.

To begin, ground yourself and make sure you have the strong, clear intention that you wish to open the light for the spirit to cross over to their rightful next place. Next, I visualize a thin, vertical line of bright white light that starts small and grows seven or eight feet in height, splitting the air in the center of where you want the portal to be. See it as the brightest light you can imagine! Like staring into the sun. I also see it as being prismatic, meaning it has a slight rainbow shimmer around the edges. Slowly and steadily, the thin line widens and grows until it's wide open and welcoming. The light is warm and gentle, and it even, on occasion, emits a pleasant sound. Some folks see it as swirling or pulsing, but for me it's always just a gauzy pillow of radiant white light. From there, the spirit is welcome to enter. Once the spirit has gone through, you may close the light behind them by visualizing the light shrinking back to nothing. You may also wish to state a time limit for the portal. If you want it to remain open for twenty-four hours, or several days, you can simply state it clearly in your mind or out loud to set the timer on it. This is helpful when you feel there may be other human spirits around that wish to cross over as well.

An alternative visualization that I see used a lot is the door. Both of these work wonderfully, but you may find one or the other easier for you. The door visualization is similar, beginning with a thin line of bright white light. This time, though, it's a thin line that grows to form the edges of a rectangle. This ends up creating the image of a door with bright white light blasting out of the cracks around the frame. Then, with intention, push the door open, revealing the light. From there, the spirit is free to cross over, and you can close the door behind them.

And that is it. Do not be deceived by its simplicity; it really is that easy. However, you may find that some ghosts will hesitate for one reason or another and that others will be so paralyzed by fear when it comes to crossing that they will refuse. It's at this point that you have a couple of options. My favorite, and the most helpful, is to ask the spirit if there is someone on the other side whom they trust. This is pretty much always a loved one, such as a grandmother, a best friend, or, on one occasion, a much-loved dog. Once you know whom they wish to see, you can ask their loved one's spirit to come back through the light to help escort them across. These helpful spirits are often ready and very willing to assist, and I've never had a problem getting one to come through. When they arrive, it's really beautiful, and they usually take it from there, helping the earthbound ghost through the light.

If the earthbound is an unruly or harmful spirit that is refusing to go through the light but also poses a threat, you can ask for angels to come through and grab them and pull them through. Sounds a little weird, but it does in fact work. I've also blasted a few through the light with sheer force of will. It's always best, though, to counsel the spirit and get them to go through willingly.

Ritual

CROSSING-OVER CEREMONY

Usually, you'll be popping the light open at will in order to move spirits through, but sometimes it's nice to dress up the process in order to make it special. Whether you choose to do this every time or only on occasion is up to you. I also recommend doing this if you are having trouble with the above technique, as adding ritual can make the process easier when you are first starting. When working with locations that have many earthbound entities, this is a good way to get them all through.

You'll need four white tealight candles, one white plate, holy water or olive oil, incense, salt, and a tall glass of water.

Begin by saying a prayer and making sure that you have all your protections in order. Turn out all the lights in the home and light the incense. Anoint each candle with your choice of holy water or olive oil and arrange them into a diamond shape on the plate, with the glass of water in the center, and set it somewhere safe, such as on a sturdy table or somewhere out of the way on a tile floor. Sit before the plate and get comfortable. Ground yourself and call upon your helping spirits and guides. When you feel ready, state your intention or say a prayer, and then begin to visualize the candles radiating beautiful white light. The glow intensifies and drifts upward, collecting over the glass and growing brighter and brighter until there is a brilliant, pulsating portal of beautiful white light suspended above the plate. See the light produced by the candles continuing to feed the portal, keeping it open. Once it's open and glowing beautifully, begin to call to the *human* spirits that are stuck in the home. Invite them to move closer to the light and its warmth and comfort. Let them know that it's open to all of them who wish to cross over, and tell them there is no reason to be afraid. As a folk worker, I will often open a Bible to Psalm 23 and place it at the base of the portal with the candles and read it aloud. It brings peace to restless spirits and repels negative entities.

As you do this, you may get the sense that a crowd has gathered around you, or you may feel the air become heavy or start to buzz. Keep speaking to the spirits, encouraging them to go through the light. The heaviness will dissipate as they cross over. Once you feel they have all gone through, mix a little salt into a bowl of water and go around the home, letting any stragglers know that it's time to either move on through the light or vacate the premises. After you've given ample warning, begin to cleanse the space with sprinkles of salt water.

Fracturing

On some occasions when human spirits are sent through the light, a piece of them will splinter off and remain behind. I call this "fracturing." Usually, the thing that gets left behind is something that they need to let go of in order to cross over. The light has a way of purifying and filtering these things from people and will occasionally reject parts of them as they go through it. The pieces that are left behind are usually unsavory in nature, such as their anger, their trauma, their addiction, or even their mental illness. Most folks who have ever had a loved one who was an addict understand that a person can seem like two different people: their sober self, and the person they become when they are using. This dual personality goes deep into the spirit, and that "other person" whom they become often gets left behind when they go into the light because it's not really a part of them; it is just something they've acquired in this life. Sometimes this rejected part of them is large enough to make a whole, functioning spirit right out of the gate. Other times, the rejected parts are just small shards of sadness or regret, or something else they had to leave behind in order to cross over. These broken pieces can grow—either on their own or by gathering with other pieces—into what will often seem like an earthbound human spirit, but it is just a shadow of them. These are often quite disruptive, as they are only the unhealed parts of the person.

To prevent these from becoming a problem, I recommend doing a thorough cleanse of a space after a spirit has been sent through the light. The shards are harder to get rid of after they have time to grow into active spirit entities, so it's best to get them early. Also, stick around to make sure you get the sense that the spirit has gone completely. I've had instances in which only half of the spirit seems to go through and half has stayed on our side. Sometimes they need another talking-to—or a good shove—to get them completely through the light. If the fracture has been allowed to grow into a fully active spirit, you have a couple of options. Sometimes if you try a second time, these left-behind pieces will be accepted by the light if there is enough humanity left in them. However, sometimes the light will not take them, and in these cases you'll need to banish them and then protect the home to prevent them from coming back. These leftover shadow pieces are susceptible to banishment through your usual cleansing methods like burning herbs and resins, but you can also try salt. Each case will be a little different, so feel free to experiment.

Are Earthbound Spirits Dangerous?

This is a question I receive a lot: "Can ghosts hurt me?" The answer is yes, *if you let them*. While earthbound spirits may not hold as much power as other entities, they can indeed cause a problem for the living. While some of them are understandably angry, others are simply bad people who wish to hurt others. Murderers, rapists, abusers, and sadists must die at some point, just like the rest of us, and these are usually the ones who wish to stay behind the most. Even those without criminal records can be quite vindictive and choose to cause harm to the living. But how do they do it?

Physical Danger

Though most folks believe that only negative entities can cause big physical disturbances, this is untrue. Even earthbound human spirits can be quite powerful when it comes to physical interaction. This includes pushing, shoving, hitting, tackling, and the moving of objects, such as knocking items off a shelf or throwing them across a room. This takes practice, but some earthbounds become quite good at it.

In other instances, people have reported sexual encounters with spirits of the dead. While some folks willingly engage in sex with ghosts, there have been numerous reports of sexual assault perpetrated by them as well, as in the famous case of Doris Bither, often referred to as "the Entity haunting" after the 1978 book *The Entity* based on her case and the subsequent 1982 film of the same name. She was sexually assaulted almost daily by three spirits while living in her home in Culver City, California. This type of phenomenon is rare, but it does happen, and it's not strictly limited to ghosts, either. Other entities can do this as well, and we'll talk more on that later.

Influence on the Living

Earthbound spirits have a curious ability to affect the living. We already know that they get their energy from being around us, but some will actively target humans for feeding, causing them to quickly become tired, depressed, or irritable. Sometimes their presence may cause disease, especially if that spirit itself is sick in some way. Other times they may play on the emotions of the living, causing turmoil in relationships by flaring tempers and whispering bad thoughts in people's ears. Ghosts with addictions may pass on their habits to the living by coaxing them to drink or smoke or do drugs. All of these things become much worse and much more dangerous if the ghost is allowed to attach to a living person.

Attachments

It's rare that an earthbound human spirit will just attach to you out of the blue for no reason. Usually, that only happens when either your defenses are way down (like if you're blackout drunk) or if you've invited them or opened yourself up in some manner. Most of the time, however, it takes a while for the spirit to get close enough to form an attachment.

Once the spirit is attached, they can wreak all kinds of havoc. From there, the spirit may drain your energy, make you sick, influence your thoughts and emotions, and change your habits. People with attachments may feel lethargic, anxious, or tired, like they've been carrying something heavy around on their back. They may suddenly be quite irritable or begin to drink heavily and use drugs in a manner that is unlike them. Their health may decline dramatically without medical explanation, or they may develop sudden mental health issues like paranoia or major depression.

Removing an Attached Earthbound Human Spirit

Removing an attached human spirit can be a tricky business and should not be undertaken lightly. These spirits will often lash out and can injure the person attempting the removal, as well as the host. If you decide to do this, be sure to have some extra supplies, a plan B, and your protections in place. I recommend saying a prayer before you begin as well.

You can go about this in a couple of ways. Each of these methods can be effective as a stand-alone treatment, but you may want to mix and match. The important part is to get the affected person to declare out loud that they are breaking all ties with the ghost and that the spirit is no longer welcome in their energy field. This is the key to being successful. Not only does this facilitate the process by setting an intention, but spirits must respect certain boundaries that we put up as sovereign beings. Consciously deciding not to let a spirit interact with you is a huge part of freeing and guarding yourself from them. When you're done with the removal, be sure to cleanse the whole home to make sure that nothing is still hanging around.

Ritual

SALT BATH

An effective hands-off remedy for an attached human spirit is a good, stout salt bath. I like this because it's something the client can do on their own and you don't have to be involved. In a standard-size bathtub I would add about 3 cups of salt. (I like coarse sea salt, but they can use what they have.) If your client would like to do half Epsom salts, that is fine, but be sure to have them use at least half regular salt. I prefer to pray over both the water and the salt, first separately, and then once more after they've been mixed. The client should soak in this for at least fifteen minutes and declare with feeling that they are releasing themselves from all spirits of the dead, and ask that their guides and guardians remove the spirit and take them far away. This should take off any loose or newly formed attachments. When they are done, they should blot themselves dry with a soft towel and anoint themselves with protective oils, especially on the back of the neck and between the shoulder blades.

To increase the power of this bath, you may have them add cleansing herbs like hyssop, rosemary, and rue. For cutting power, they can add limes or lemons. For tough cases, you can have them use an infusion of a plant called Espanta Muerto, which banishes earthbound spirits. Some botanicas will sell "Ghost Chaser" bath crystals made with Espanta Muerto as well, and I've been told they do the trick.

Ritual

SMOKE BATH

Some types of smoke will chase away the dead. You'll want to use something gross like garlic or garlic skins, or if you're really serious, you can reach for asafoetida. This will undoubtedly send them packing, but it will also be uncomfortable for you and your client. If you are looking for something more pleasant, plants like rue can also be used. You may also burn Espanta Muerto, or Tibetan ghost purging incense. Some botanicas sell "Ghost Chaser" incense too; just make sure it's derived from real plants. If you're going the loose-herb route, I recommend burning it on a good-size charcoal disk nestled on top of a bowl full of salt. Don't forget to have the client declare out loud that they break all attachments with the spirit and no longer want the spirit on or near them.

Now, the method of administering the smoke bath will vary depending on your commitment level and your resources. You may thoroughly waft the smoke over them, or take them into an enclosed space. This can be anything from a small room or closet to a makeshift tent. The latter you can do by throwing a sheet over the person and the backs of some chairs, creating a little space to fill with smoke. It works in a pinch, but your client may look at you funny. (Also be sure not to accidentally catch the sheet on fire. You're working with hot charcoal, so be mindful.) Whatever you choose, you'll want to really smoke it up in there. As you do so, have the person declare—calmly but with feeling—that they are releasing the spirit. When you or your client feels the spirit detach, open the door or cast off the sheet and throw open some windows to let them free. Be sure to cleanse the home afterward, to make sure they're truly gone. Even then, I still prescribe a salt bath to the client, and I take one myself when I get home. It doesn't hurt to be thorough. When the client is finished, anoint them with protective oils.

Banishing a Ghost

The only way to really resolve a haunting caused by an earthbound human spirit is to get them to go through the light (see above); otherwise, you're just moving the problem around instead of truly fixing it. However, most folks will want a plan B or an alternative. In my day, I've seen a lot of folks try many different things to get rid of a ghost, and only some of them work. Here we'll go over the things I've found most effective.

Salt: Salt tends to be rather effective when it comes to repelling spirits of the dead. It can be employed either in its natural crystallized form or in a liquid form like salt water. When I'm done cleansing a home, I like to add just a small pinch of salt to every corner of every room to protect the home and clear away anything that might be lingering. Small sachets of salt placed around the home are believed to "dry out" spirits as well, causing them to leave.

Unpleasant Smoke: Some plant allies and resins produce vibrations, or clear away certain energies, making conditions unfavorable for ghosts to stay. Some of these accomplish this goal by simply being unbearable; therefore, burning irritating things like hot peppers, garlic, or garlic skins, as well as stinky powders like asafoetida, may indeed chase away a ghost. Other types have special energetic abilities that make them natural expellers. Rue, ethically sourced white sage, thyme, and rosemary are all exceptionally good at this and may be helpful in sending away ghosts. Remember to use these with strong, clear intention and power.

Lilac: Lilac has a beautiful energy, and it has long been believed to exorcise ghosts from a space. I like this method because it's very gentle but still effective. Place fresh lilac blooms with some salt on a plate in every room while asking that the ghosts leave. This can be combined with the crossing-over ceremony found earlier in this chapter.

Force of Will: This is something that takes a little practice, but you can indeed force a human spirit out of a space using your own personal will—no tools, just your mind. When learning, it's best to have a set technique that you work with. For instance, when I was getting the hang of this, I would visualize a sturdy brick wall in front of me and then I would push it toward the spirit, forcing them out of the space. You may also come up with an incantation that helps you focus. In my culture (Mexican), we often suggest swearing profusely at the spirit to accomplish this. It all does the same thing; with enough focus and energy, you can banish a spirit too. Just make sure to really mean it and really push with your energy.

CHAPTER 8
The Poltergeist Phenomenon

The most misunderstood haunting is the poltergeist. The name itself is a misnomer and is commonly translated from German as "noisy ghost." However, a poltergeist isn't a spirit, at least not in the usual sense. The phenomenon is believed to be caused by unintentional PK (psychokinesis) on the part of the "haunted" person(s). Or, in general terms, one or more living humans in the home is causing the activity unintentionally by throwing off loads of psychic energy. This creates a cloud of chaotic or destructive energy that is fed by the creator(s). This theory also helps explain the erratic and nonsensical nature of a poltergeist.

Typically, this type of haunting centers around a person who is in the early or middle stages of puberty, commonly adolescent girls. This type of activity can be seen in male children and adults as well, but it's less common. The reason for the preference for adolescent girls is believed to be a matter of energy. In puberty, the body goes through many intense chemical changes, which give off energy. There is also a lot of emotional energy associated with adolescent girls, and this combination often packs a wallop. The energy must go somewhere. Like static electricity, it can only build up so much before it throws a spark. Instead of a spark, though, you get stacked furniture, objects that fly across the room, drawers opening, and fires starting. Most people grow out of it, though, and poltergeists are often short-lived, lasting anywhere from a few weeks to a couple of years.

While we know very little about this phenomenon, in my experience, poltergeists tend to gain momentum and eventually can detach from their host and roam freely for varying lengths of time. For instance, though they tend to follow a specific person, there may be activity in the home even when the person is not there. This will often mask the presence of other spirits or entities that may be present as well. If the poltergeist is allowed to gain enough energy and momentum, it may detach from its source and become a free-floating, self-sustained mass of chaotic energy. However, even these don't tend to last very long.

Poltergeists often exude a mischievous and somewhat child-like personality—no doubt a product of their usual source, young people. This can make them difficult to deal with, but also quite comical on occasion. They tend to present as sentient beings and are prone to back-sass and pranks, and it's good to keep a sense of humor when working with them. Other times, though, poltergeists can be quite insidious and produce some chilling effects. I've found the latter to be most common in poltergeists caused by grown adults. You'll come to realize that poltergeists take on some of the personality or baggage of those who cause them. This adds to their mysterious nature and will be something you'll have to keep in mind while trying to diagnose the problem. For instance, the poltergeist may react badly to religious iconography, but this doesn't necessarily mean it is "demonic" in nature. The person causing it may have deeply held religious trauma, and therefore the poltergeist will have an aversion to such things.

Though this type of activity is often caused by pubescent girls, it can be created in a few different ways. I once sat on a couch across from a family who was describing some rather disturbing poltergeist phenomena happening in their home. All of them were over the age of thirty, and about five of them lived in the same big house together. They were an assorted bunch of cousins and an aunt who had decided to cohabitate out of necessity. While none of them were exactly a prime candidate for poltergeist activity, being in a room with them all together was very telling. None of them could get out more than a few sentences before being rudely met with bickering and arguing from the others. These moments of friction would quickly escalate to yelling and screaming, and we had to ask them to behave like adults more than once. The dysfunctional family before me was creating their own intense emotional energy that was collecting in the home like static electricity, waiting to discharge in the form of a thrown object or a sound.

Undoubtedly, a poltergeist will be one of the stranger types of haunting that you work with. Their odd and erratic behavior defies definition or categorization. Not to mention, their tendency to coincide with other hauntings often adds to their enigmatic nature and makes them that much harder to understand. Determining where a poltergeist ends and another haunting begins can be very tricky. This is why you should take your time and be thorough.

Identifying a Poltergeist

Poltergeists are characterized by odd disturbances that often seem to occur without purpose and make little to no sense. Though some can be quite powerful, the activity is often simply inconvenient, mischievous, or just plain weird. The way we generally differentiate between a haunting and a poltergeist is that a haunting most often happens around a location while a poltergeist happens around a person. And though it may affect others in the home, a poltergeist will center on what we call the "poltergeist agent" (see page 135), which you will have to identify as well. An example of this would be a famous poltergeist event that happened in the London borough of Enfield some years ago: it was documented that when the poltergeist agent (a young girl named Janet) walked through the kitchen, the drawers would suddenly pull out as she passed. That's not typical of other types of hauntings. Beyond that, there are several other telltale signs that will help you identify this type of haunting.

Stacked and Moving Objects

The hallmark of a poltergeist is the spontaneous stacking of objects, seemingly of their own volition. This includes books, pictures, lamps, and pieces of furniture like chairs and tables. These items often form themselves into a tower or a pyramid shape and will occasionally defy physics. I've seen a line of forks balanced vertically end to end, frozen in place.

Apart from stacking, moving objects are quite common in this type of haunting. This includes objects flying across the room of their own accord and furniture and home decor rearranging itself on its own. It's frequent that all the family photos will be turned around to face the wall or the pantry will reorganize itself by color or size. Potted plants may move themselves around the home at random. Couches may be thrown across the room. These events can range from miniscule to big outbursts, like all the drawers in your kitchen pulling out at once or all the furniture arranging itself on the ceiling. Poltergeists like to flagrantly disregard the laws of physics.

Fires

Poltergeists have the concerning habit of starting fires. Luckily, they rarely burn down a home or cause any damage. Instead, they tend to create small, controlled blazes that only affect a single object. For instance, I've heard stories of single balls of tissues going up in flames only to go out moments later, and one specific teddy bear in a pile that ignites for several seconds but is left unharmed once it's put out.

Apports and Teleports

An apport occurs when an object materializes out of thin air. One of the most well-documented cases, the Enfield poltergeist (mentioned previously), reported that tiny blue marbles that did not belong to the family would appear out of nowhere and suddenly shoot across the room at high speeds. What's weirder is that they were hot to the touch, and after colliding with an object (whether that was a wall or someone's head), they wouldn't bounce when hitting the ground. They'd simply hit the floor and stick. Other times, a poltergeist may produce other random objects at will, such as flowers or coins.

Similarly, this type of phenomenon will also engage in teleportation. Objects from locked boxes and other closed-off spaces will disappear and reappear outside of their containers. For instance, I once heard a story about a poltergeist that had a thing for eggs. It would open the fridge and float them all out one at a time. When the person in the home closed the fridge door on it one day, she watched as each egg slowly materialized outside of the fridge before drifting away.

Wet Spots

Similar to apports, poltergeists are notorious for leaving puddles. Sometimes large pools of standing water or soaked spots in the carpet will be found with no apparent cause. A lot of folks call plumbers in this situation but are often met with puzzled looks and a shrug.

Indoor Weather Events

Yes, you read that correctly. These are rare, but poltergeists are known to occasionally pull off an indoor weather event. Ever had it start raining in the living room? It's not unheard of for rain or even snow (or snowlike material) to begin falling from somewhere near the ceiling. Gusts of wind and even small cyclones have been reported.

Inappropriate Mayhem

I wasn't sure what to label the act of smearing feces—usually of a suspicious origin—on the wall to spell out rude words, but "inappropriate mayhem" sounded about right. It's not always feces, though; sometimes it's some sort of food, paint, or mud. Poltergeists have an affinity for crude language and will frequently spell out curse words or draw dirty images on walls or furniture using any messy substance they can find.

Mimicking Voices

A rather unsettling thing that poltergeists will do is mimic people's voices. Folks will hear their spouse or roommate calling to them from another room, and when they go to see what they want, no one is there and the person they heard usually isn't even in the home. On one occasion, I had a family—the same family who couldn't stop fighting—experience full doppelgangers. Each member of the household had met with a double of another family member. For example, Lucy would be standing in the kitchen and Amy would come in. They'd have a brief but very real conversation, and then Amy would go upstairs. Then, suddenly, the *real* Amy would come through the front door, returning from the grocery store. The Amy that Lucy had a conversation with was nowhere to be found upstairs. In other instances, one of the family members might be standing outside and wave to someone inside the house who was looking out a window at them. A moment later, they'd get a call from the person they just saw, saying they were on their way home from work. Each member of the family had experienced at least one of these encounters.

Make no mistake, many entities have this ability, and while it *is* a sign of poltergeist activity, it can also be caused by more sinister forces looking to gain closer access to the family. I urge you to take this type of activity seriously and do your due diligence in checking the house for other possible causes.

The Poltergeist Agent

The person who creates the poltergeist is known as the "agent" of the poltergeist. As discussed before, the agent is most commonly a child who is bordering on puberty. They tend to be very bright for their age and are often young girls. However, boys, as well as full-grown adults, can also be poltergeist agents, especially when they are under massive pressure or trying to deal with big emotional issues. For instance, adults going through a divorce or dealing with the death of a close family member may cause activity. No matter the age or gender of the agent, this existential pressure seems to be a key factor in igniting the activity, and it's common to find this phenomenon in homes of families who are experiencing some sort of turmoil, like divorce, or have children who are under high pressure to perform academically. Though many folks can produce this type of activity, it's believed that those who produce spectacular poltergeist phenomena are special. Many of the famous laboratory-tested psychokinetics, such as Nina Kulagina of Russia and Joasia Gajewski of Poland, were former poltergeist agents.[2] This lends further credence to the theory that these are created by unintentional PK activity.

Addressing a Poltergeist

Most poltergeists will resolve themselves in a few months to a couple of years. However, most folks are not willing to wait that long. Resolving a poltergeist is actually quite simple. In the case of children causing the activity, simply telling them they are causing it will often cause it to cease immediately.[3] Let me explain: Have you ever done something super cool accidentally, like lazily tossing a basketball over your shoulder only to have it swish through the net? Amazing, right? But now try to do it again on purpose. Not in a million years would you be able to recreate it. Same thing applies to telling folks they are causing the haunting: once they know, the whole thing comes to a screeching halt. The rest of the family should also do what they can to lessen the pressure on the poltergeist agent, as this is also a main contributing factor.

Adult poltergeist agents, on the other hand, will need to seek some sort of professional help, such as personal therapy or group relationship counseling, depending on if they are the sole agent or part of a dysfunctional group creating the disturbance. Once their personal drama dies down, the poltergeist should weaken and eventually dissipate. In any case, it may take a little time—a few weeks to a couple of months—for the haunting to completely stop, especially if it has gone on for a while and has gained momentum. Eventually, the activity will dissipate. I would also recommend

2. Michael Clarkson, *The Poltergeist Phenomenon: An In-Depth Investigation into Floating Beds, Smashing Glass, and Other Unexplained Disturbances* (Pompton Plains, NJ: New Page Books, 2011), 19–20.

3. Loyd Auerbach, *ESP, Hauntings and Poltergeists: A Parapsychologist's Handbook* (Self-published, CreateSpace Independent Publishing Platform, 2016), 267.

regular cleansing to release any excess energy. Some powerful poltergeist agents may continue to show PK activity for the duration of their lifetime.

Exercise

GROUNDING THE SPACE

Something that can help ease the activity associated with a poltergeist is a good grounding of the home. This can help stabilize and release some of the excess energy. You can do this in a few different ways, but you'll need four objects. You can use heavy rocks, such as stones pulled from a river (be sure to ask for permission and pay the river for them), potted plants or potted indoor trees, or grounding crystals, such as obsidian. Whichever you choose, you'll want to place one in each of the four corners of the home on the inside. Each time you place one, ask that it ground the home and absorb some of the excess energy and send it into the earth. I usually visualize that each item grows a big root into the ground that the energy can travel down.

CHAPTER 9
Inhuman Spirits

Many folks believe that the only things on the other side are ghosts, angels, and demons, but that's far from the truth. The fourth category of haunting you might come across is the infamous "inhuman spirit." These are often the most feared and least understood beings in this spectrum. The world of inhuman spirits is vast and encompasses the Fae, elementals (gnomes, nymphs, merfolk, and so on), animal spirits, shadow people, demonic entities, predatory and parasitic entities, thoughtforms, forest spirits, and much, *much* more! Just as nature is flush with many diverse species, so is the spirit world. Each is unique and has a different purpose. Not all of them are evil; though some can and do harm people, it's not always with evil intent. Much like the spider who eats the fly: the spider isn't evil, but it does have to eat. This is a category of spirit that one must handle carefully, and you must be sure not to make any agreements with them. Many of them can be tricky at best and nasty at worst. If faced with this type of entity, reach out to a local professional for help if you feel you are in over your head. I will warn you that this area can get a bit dicey and will test the resiliency of any investigator who dares to venture in their direction. This is where you get to come face-to-face with things you never even thought could exist in your wildest dreams—or your worst nightmares.

In September of 2019, I was asked to investigate an abandoned wing of a mall in Portland. The security guards were the ones who requested the investigation and let us in after hours. These were all large, fully grown men with years of experience in security, and they were scared out of their wits. Their accounts of the activity included lights going on and off and doors opening and closing on their own. They frequently heard disembodied voices speaking to them out of the shadows. Two female spirits were seen regularly, including a woman in white as well as an eight-foot-tall, old and decaying nude woman. Not to mention the small, green-eyed creatures wearing cloaks and hoods that had been spotted multiple times in an odd, round room that looked, well … a bit like a spaceship, I won't lie. As I said before, this stuff gets weird.

While the following list does not encompass all the beings and creatures that belong to the category of inhuman spirits, it will familiarize you with some of the more common ones you are likely to encounter. Negative entities belong in this category but will be discussed in the following chapter.

The Fae

You'll have a lot of wild conversations with folks when it comes to this work. However, I've never felt crazier than when I first had to tell someone that their problem wasn't a ghost, but fairies. Yup, fairies. These tricky little bastards will hide your keys, steal shiny objects, and cause general mayhem. Usually, it's small pranks, but if provoked they may escalate to more diabolical activity. Many folks identify this type of haunting based on the style of activity as well as the presence of small pinpoints of light seen flying across the room. I've experienced this myself, and it is quite startling when you see it. To address this type of issue, I recommend building the fairies a little home somewhere outside, such as in the backyard. Using sticks, branches, and stones, you can build a small structure and fill it with neat things like shiny coins or pretty sea-shells. Let them know it is for them, and leave them a little treat like honey or plant some flowers around it. This usually clears things up pretty quickly.

Elementals

Elementals don't tend to cause a problem, but they do show up in this work every now and again. This is a broad category of creature that includes any spirits related to one of the four elements. These are things like gnomes (earth), sylphs (air), all manner of nymphs and sprites, and forest spirits (see below). You won't come across these on most of your standard investigations, but sometimes they do get involved. They are very tricky and should be handled very carefully—and only when necessary. Be sure to check all the fine print before agreeing to anything.

Forest Spirits

A homeowner emailed our team with a request for a resolve and included a photo of a bloody mess that had been left on his porch. He had recently built his gorgeous two-story home in a heavily forested area in lower Washington state. This meant the removal of some timber and a lot of noisy construction. The thing that spurred him to send us a message was the grizzly spectacle that he found on his porch. To this day, I'm not certain what it was. It was clearly regurgitated, like something had come up onto his porch and thrown up a bellyful of blood along with a piece of something. It looked a bit like an organ or a part of a small, skinless animal. I only got to see a picture of it. We couldn't get out there for another week, and by that time he had thrown it away but left the mess. Trapped between the wooden slats of his porch were chunks of whatever this critter had been. They were still gooey, and the blood was still wet. It seemed like the incident had happened within the last hour, not over a week ago. It had been hot, too. The blood and remains should have been jerky by then, but they had refused to dry or decay. Some believe that evil things refuse to rot, and I've been told that often things like animals used in satanic rituals will decay much more slowly than usual. Some folks think it's a rude imitation of incorrupt saints, which also don't decay as a sign of their holiness. While that is a possible explanation, we must remember that we don't really know.

The man was also seeing creatures in the woods, including a very tall, black, hairy creature with red eyes. He described it as a Bigfoot type of shape, but all black, like a shadow. He saw it crossing his driveway when he went to take out the trash. It was broad daylight. His grandson, who stayed there often, would repeatedly wake up in the middle of the night to find a tall, hairy creature peeking into his second-story bedroom. While this was a multiple-haunting scenario, the disgruntled forest spirits were some of the scariest I've seen.

The world of forest spirits is a daunting one. I personally would rather go up against a negative entity any day than face off with a forest spirit, especially one that is corrupt or angry. These creatures are immensely powerful, and they are also very strange. They are wild, unkempt, and unruly. They are often crooked, hairy, or misshapen in appearance. Luckily, you don't come across them very often, except when they are disturbed, so let's look at the most common ways these hauntings are brought on.

Construction or Clear-Cutting

First, doing any sort of construction that involves disturbing the forest is generally a bad idea. This riles the spirits up. I recommend doing a ceremony and offering some natural gifts to the earth, such as smoke, shells, and tobacco, before starting any new construction. Introduce yourself to the spirits there, let them know what you plan to do with the property, and wait for a response. If you've already angered them, my advice would be to try to say you are sorry. Make offerings to the forest spirits, explain yourself, and apologize profusely. Planting native fruit trees is also believed to help appease them. You then have to hope that they accept. You can't cleanse these spirits away. They have rights to the land, and you are a trespasser—which brings us to my next point.

Trespassing

Second, trespassing can really set them off as well. Did you find a beautiful blue pool tucked away from view while out on a hike? Think twice before diving into it. There are secret places that belong to forest spirits, and human presence in them is often seen as a desecration. We leave trash and mark trees and disturb the natural things growing there. This is unwelcome in their world. If you come across a beautiful natural wonder that you want to interact with, ask permission first. If you get the sense that you are unwelcome, move on quickly. If you feel that you are accepted there, do your best to behave. Respect the place, pick up all your trash, and don't overstay your welcome. If you find that you or a client have incurred the wrath of forest spirits by trespassing, the best thing to do is apologize. Go back, make offerings *that won't pollute the area*, and explain yourself. Hopefully, they will forgive you.

Stealing

Third, taking things from these places is considered taboo. We don't own everything, and not all things found in nature are free. This is especially true of things taken from sacred sites like the ruins of ancient temples and even from places like volcanoes. Taking rocks or other souvenirs often leads to horrendous luck, spiritual sickness, and even hauntings. The only way to fix this is to give back whatever was taken with sincere apologies. Always make sure to ask permission before taking these things, even something as insignificant as a rock.

Shadow People

Shadow people are really common, and you will likely come across them frequently in this work. What are they? Well, no one really knows. In my experience, they tend to gather when someone in the home is going through a dark period, such as grieving the death of a loved one or going through a period of depression or anxiety. They seem to be attracted to the sadness more than the fear, but they will feed on fear as well. Their presence can often make depression or anxiety worse, but in my experience they don't tend to be too aggressive. They travel in groups and are frequently seen out of the corner of the eye. Shadow people tend to be attracted to (and possibly cause) sleep paralysis as well. Many folks report their presence either during or just before a bout of sleep paralysis. This category of entity defies a lot of attempts at definition, because folks often perceive a wide variety of supernatural creatures as shadowy figures, which then get lumped together with what we call "shadow people."

Clyde, the Top Hat Man

I first came across the entity I lovingly call Clyde several years ago in a very haunted bar in downtown Portland. I was called there to help with an active haunting that included a male figure a lot of patrons had repeatedly seen. I got to have a conversation with this spirit, and let me tell you, he left an impression. The first time I met Clyde, he was wearing a purple tuxedo with tails, gloves, a bowtie, spats—the works. While speaking with him, I began to realize that something wasn't right about his appearance. His skin didn't seem to fit right. It was like he was wearing a body suit made of human skin that always needed adjusting. Then I noticed how yellow his eyes were. When I realized what was going on, I confronted him. "You're not a human spirit, are you?" I said flatly, letting him know I was on to his game. He responded by smiling. As he did so, his mouth opened to an inhuman width and exposed rows of jagged shark teeth. The effect was chilling, to say the least.

After our first encounter, I came across this spirit again and again. His appearances were so common that I gave him the name Clyde. I do this sometimes, because giving these entities a generic human name—Bob, Carl, Fred, Jenny—can make them seem much less scary, if not comical. Eventually, it got to the point that I decided to Google his description and see if others had come into contact with him as well. Turns out, they had. He's well-known in the world of hauntings, and many know him as "the Top Hat Man" or simply "the Hat Man." By far the most dapper of entities, Clyde is almost always seen wearing a suit and some sort of hat. It's usually a top hat or a fedora, but it's also common to hear of him wearing something else, like a bowler hat or a wide-brimmed Amish-style hat. He's tall, thin, and sometimes crooked in posture. He likes to show up looking very human, but he can't hide once you know. Clyde also has a thing for mirrors. Many people will see him in the reflection of mirrors, or he will seem to "live" in mirrors.

From what I can tell, he seems to be an "upper-level" version of shadow people. I often think of him like their manager. He tends to be attracted to the same things as them, like depression, sadness, and fear. His presence seems to intensify these issues as well. I don't get the impression that he is one spirit but instead a type of spirit that I've seen many versions of. I usually tell the difference between a Clyde and a well-dressed human spirit by the teeth and the eyes. Clyde tends to have off-colored eyes, such as red or yellow. His teeth and mouth area often give him away as well. He will often have sharp teeth or some other oral abnormality, such as a long, snaking tongue or no lower jaw. There is a very similar spirit from the Seneca Nation called "High Hat" who is often described as a tall, flesh-eating spirit that wears a stovepipe hat and gloves and has a mouthful of sharp teeth.

Astral Parasites

Astral parasites are extremely common. You probably have one right now and don't even know it. Like leeches, these aren't necessarily dangerous but can be a bit of nuisance. These are small creatures that attach to people and feed off their energy. I see them a little like ticks or weird starfish that latch on with little suckers. These are easily removed and are one of the reasons why having a good cleansing and protection routine in place is important. These don't just attach to the living; they attach to earthbound human spirits as well.

Exercise

REMOVING ASTRAL PARASITES

Astral parasites can be removed in all kinds of ways, such as an aura flush (see page 15), smoke cleansing, or taking a cleansing bath. Sometimes you may not have time for one of these and will have to remove them by hand. To remove these from a living person, you'll want to begin by grounding yourself. Bring your hands to prayer position at your heart center and state your intention before visualizing white fire engulfing your hands. Using your dominant hand, reach into the person's aura just a few inches from their body and slowly sweep down, stopping anywhere you feel an energetic anomaly. This may feel like a bump, a bit of darkness, a hot or cold spot, or a patch of static. When you find these, you'll want to remove them. This can be done in a few ways: you may pluck them, scoop them, or slowly draw them out and flick your hand downward toward the floor to ground the energy. Sometimes when they feel stuck, you may need to spin them. I remember watching my teacher Lane do this many times, taking her two fingers (index and middle finger) and spinning some sort of energetic anomaly until it came out like a screw. Once it comes free, flick it down toward the ground to get rid of it. When you're done, cleanse yourself and the room.

Thoughtforms

Thoughtforms are small creatures that I often see as grapefruit-sized balls of smoke. These are usually created by accident through our routine thoughts and beliefs, but they can also be created on purpose to act as a servitor. These are simply low-powered artificial spirits created by human psychic energy, a little like a wind-up toy. They don't tend to cause much of a problem but can cause some mischief or odd noises or feelings in the home. Sometimes the family will report seeing a little ball of something zooming through the air. I was once asked to look at a home in which some strange activity was happening and found a thoughtform that liked to rocket through the home at high speeds, bouncing off hard surfaces like a pinball and making a small *ping* sound. These are easily cleansed away by normal means, or you can dissolve them with some simple mental magic. Things like tulpas and egregores are much larger versions of thoughtforms.

Mimics

Mimics are some of my least favorite of all the inhuman spirits. These are entities that will pretend to be other spirits, or even living people. They seem to enjoy fooling people into thinking they are something they are not and will often push the limits of how far they can go before they are found out. Some will disguise themselves as helpful or friendly spirits in order to see how close they can get to the family. Others will mimic the voices of those living in the home in order to play tricks. The most unsettling is when they take on the full identity of a living human person and then interact with other living people face-to-face. While many mimics can be very convincing, there is always something wrong or out of place in their appearance. They can't do a perfect imitation.

Collectors

I have seen some scary things in my years doing this work. The most chilling is something I call a collector. These are inhuman spirits that will collect earthbound human spirits the same way that hunters will display the pelts and heads of their kills. The trouble is that these human earthbounds are often still conscious. Sometimes a collector will do this by posing as a fellow human spirit and forming a cultlike group, with it as the leader. Others will paralyze or incapacitate the human earthbounds and arrange them like a display in a museum. This is one of the many reasons why I often encourage earthbound spirits to cross over through the light. Once they do, they're no longer susceptible to such horrors.

Incubi and Succubi

Incubi and succubi are malevolent spirits, often classified as demons. Incubi (singular: *incubus*) are considered the males, and succubi (singular: *succubus*) are considered the females. While most negative entities feed on fear, these are unique in the way that they attack their targets sexually, usually in the night, to feed on their sexual energy. I've come across these a good handful of times in my work, so I wouldn't really call this phenomenon rare. While there are a few different entities, including human spirits, that will function in this manner, incubi and succubi are often seen by their victims as inhuman creatures. These attacks are generally not something the victim sought out; however, you'll find that many people become quite fond of their encounters with these creatures. Many report that the sex is the best they've ever had, and this makes this type of entity particularly hard to get rid of, as folks tend to welcome them right back in. If, however, you can get the victim to break their agreements with the entity and mean it, these entities can be removed by normal cleansing means. Since these fall into the category of demons, you may want to employ the help of clergy if you are having trouble.

Demons

The topic of demons is controversial, to say the least. As soon as the word *demon* is brought up in mixed company, it reliably starts an occult food fight. I'm not here to debate with you the origins of these beings or the stuff about *demon* versus *daemon*. I'll let y'all sort out the vocabulary amongst yourselves. For the sake of vernacular, I will be using the term *demon* in this book, defined as "a malevolent spiritual entity bent on possessing the living." These are a specific breed of negative entity that is very old and very powerful. Many spirits can possess humans to varying degrees, but these are the classic crucifix-hating, backward-Latin-speaking possessors, à la *The Exorcist*. While most folks will tell you these are only found in movies, you'll come to realize that they—along with fairies, gnomes, Top Hat Men, and more—are very real.

Usually, demonic possession happens in multiple phases, and the most common three are known as infestation, oppression, and finally possession. Infestation is the arrival of the entity and the phase in which it begins to make agreements. It may disguise itself as a human spirit that needs help to get the target to develop a bit of a soft spot for it. When this happens, the agreements are easy to make. Other times, the infestation will begin as a simple haunting that quickly escalates. Sometimes, if the person is willing, the entity can skip phase two and go straight to possession if the target allows it. For instance, it may be able to talk its target into letting it borrow their body for some made-up purpose. If not, it moves to oppression, which is usually a violent haunting in which the family is forced to live in fear. It's not uncommon to walk into a home suffering from oppression and find the entire family sleeping together in one room for safety. This activity is meant to wear the family down, but it will specifically target one person much more than the others. This is the person the entity is trying to exhaust and, eventually, possess. It's also usually the first person it has come into contact with.

If you catch the entity in one of the first two stages, you may be able to exorcise it yourself (see the next chapter). However, if you feel you have a legitimate case of demonic possession, I highly recommend letting professional exorcists take over for you. One of the most important things you'll learn in this work is to recognize when you are in over your head and to reach out for help. Furthermore, certain types of mental illness or medical conditions can look just like movie portrayals of possession. If you find yourself looking to take demonic cases, I highly recommend teaming up with an open-minded but highly qualified psychologist and a medical doctor, if possible.

Helpful Spirits

Not all spirits are bad; in fact, many of them are eager to help you in this work. Allying yourself with powerful spiritual forces is an absolute game changer, and there are many to choose from. Next we will discuss a few of my favorites and how they may be helpful in your work. You may do further research into these beings and say prayers to them in order to build your relationship. Then you may call upon them with strong faith, and they will come to your assistance.

Saint Michael the Archangel

Saint Michael the Archangel is a powerful defender against all evil forces. He is most frequently depicted as a soldier angel slaying a demon with his famous sword. Saint Michael is furiously energetic and is usually happy to help! In my experience, he comes across as a Dean Winchester type of personality, from the TV series *Supernatural*, ready to blast some rock music and slay some demons. Call on him for protection from all dark forces, including evil spirits and demons, and for help in chasing them out of the home.

Hekate

The goddess Hekate is a fierce spirit who rules over the dead. She is the bearer of keys and is the guardian of all gates and thresholds, which makes her excellent at locking out evil spirits and mediating what comes in and out of a space. One of her symbols is a knife, which makes her especially helpful in assisting with the removal of spiritual attachments. Her other symbol, the torch, is helpful for guiding us in dark or lost places and for escorting spirits from this world to the next. While I've always had very positive experiences with this spirit, I don't recommend asking her to stake claim to a client's home in any way. After all, she often comes with a horde of unruly spirits, and their sustained presence may further aggravate the haunting. In all other respects, though, she can be an excellent helper in this work.

Kuan Yin

Kuan Yin (sometimes spelled *Guan Yin*) is a beautiful figure from the Buddhist tradition. Her name, in long form, translates roughly to "she who hears the cries of the world," and she's most closely associated with the virtues of compassion and mercy. Her mythos ranges widely, depending on whom you speak to, but one of my most favorite stories is of her trip to the underworld. In many versions of the story, she is a human woman who has achieved great enlightenment through Buddhism but, for one reason or another, is executed by a terrible man. After her death, she is sent to the hellish landscape of the underworld, at which point—sometimes with a song, other times with her sheer presence—the fire and rock and decay of the underworld is transformed into a lush field of beautiful flowers. The imagery of her story makes her an excellent ally for compassionate cleansing and restoration work.

CHAPTER 10
Negative Entities

Any entity whose main function is to harm, manipulate, or feed off living humans falls into the category of negative entities, which makes this category quite broad. For the purposes of this chapter, we will mainly be talking about troublesome house entities and parasitic attachment entities, as they are the ones you'll run into the most. Negative entities are often terrifying in appearance, with sharp teeth, long claws, a skeletal or twisted physical build, wings, and possibly more. They can be dangerous and can harm living people if allowed. The key is *to not be afraid of them*. That is easier said than done, though, as they are built to evoke fear in their victims. They feed on fear energy and can pull many tricks to trigger this response. Remember, in this work you have to be ready to see things you never in your life thought you would.

A few years ago, I was called to a home that was experiencing an entity haunting. The house itself was on a little less than an acre of land that sat on a busy corner near downtown. It clearly needed work, or at least a fresh coat of paint, but you can't expect much from haunted houses when it comes to upkeep. The man who answered the door was in his early forties, wearing a camo jacket and a tinfoil hat. I'm not joking; it was a baseball cap covered completely with tinfoil. According to him, it kept the "demon" away.

After we got acquainted, I took the opportunity to roam the house and soon found myself in the man's bathroom, trying to get clarity on the strange buzz the home seemed to have. That's when it happened. I had been hearing a strange scuttling noise coming from the walls. I knew it wasn't a rat or some other earthly creature, because I could only hear it with my "inside ears," meaning it was spiritual or psychic in nature. The scuttling sound intensified, like a hundred tiny fingers were scratching on the inside of the bathroom wall. One by one, out of the seam where the wall and ceiling met, hundreds of large black spiders poured out and formed a river going down the wall, out of the bathroom, and into the living room. I was startled, but I knew they were not real spiders but instead a psychic impression. I followed them out into the hall, where I watched them skitter into the living room and begin to pile on top of one another until they formed a thin, black-robed figure that loomed eerily behind the man, who was still jabbering away at our lead psychic. The figure stayed there for a moment, breathing down the man's neck until it noticed me watching it. With an irritated sigh, it disintegrated back into a river of spiders, which snaked their way across the carpet and under another door—a door the man had said was "nothing," but in reality, it was another room, one in which the entity had created a nest.

You'll come to find that some folks are invested in protecting their entities, either of their own volition or due to the influence of the spirit. Though they say they want an exorcism, many just want others to come around and experience their phenomena. As we went about the task of removing this spirit, the man seemed more interested in talking animatedly about the "really neat" things it had been doing around the home. Once we were done and felt that it had finally been removed, we packed up and left. All of us had a heaviness in the pit of our stomachs. We all knew that the exorcism wouldn't last and that the entity would be back in the home in a matter of weeks, if not days. He liked the activity too much to let it go.

About five or six years later, I was standing in line at a local ghost-hunting conference when I began to hear a man behind me telling everyone around him about his "demon." I just sort of rolled my eyes until he began describing the home and using our names. I turned around to find the same man, standing with a digital camera in hand and proudly showing off photos of his "demon" to the other people in line with him. He talked about it and showed it to folks the way proud grandparents show wallet photos of their honor-roll grandkids to anyone who will hold still long enough. To this day, the entity still inhabits the home.

Identifying a Negative-Entity Haunting

Usually, a negative entity is quite easy to spot in a home. It tends to be stronger and a lot more aggressive than your usual run-of-the-mill haunting. And while it may target one or two people in the home, generally the activity is felt by all. It wants the people in the home to be scared, because it feeds on fear.

A Sense of Dread and Discomfort

Generally, the first thing people notice is that the home begins to feel different. People may feel a growing sense of dread or discomfort, like they're being watched or like they don't belong there anymore. Certain rooms or places may suddenly begin to give people "the creeps," or they may find themselves avoiding certain places in the home because they find them to be uncomfortable. They may also feel the hair on the back of their neck stand up when they are alone or feel watched by an unidentified presence.

Odd Animal Behavior

Pets and other animals are quite attuned to the spirit world. Therefore, they are often the first to notice when something is amiss when it comes to hauntings. If your pet suddenly begins to avoid a certain area of the home or begins to act unusually aggressive toward a certain area or person, there may be cause for paranormal concern. Usually, I look to dogs more often for this kind of confirmation, because cats, well, they'll just stare into the corner with the fires of Satan in their eyes for hours on end for no real reason.

Growling Noises

While poltergeists and earthbound spirits may do a great deal of strange things, they don't tend to growl. Clients with inhuman negative entities tend to report growling or other strange, animalistic noises. I once came upon a house that reportedly made "howler-monkey-like screeches" in the middle of the night.

Minions

Something I make a point of looking for is the presence of something I call "minions." These are small shadow creatures resembling what most would refer to as "imps." Usually when I'm trying to describe them, I pull up a picture of "the Heartless" from a video game series called *Kingdom Hearts*. They stand anywhere from a few inches to a couple of feet high and can be quite nasty. Often the client will off-handedly mention that their haunting includes something small and black that seems to dart around the home. They'll say, "It's like a cat or something, but we don't have a cat!" Their presence is concerning because these small creatures often arrive alongside something much larger and much nastier. They are a bit like remora that follow sharks around. They are scavengers that like to feed on the energy produced by the entity haunting. The negative entity they serve will occasionally send them to wreak havoc in the home in the form of bothersome activity, like biting or scratching, or petty theft like stealing your car keys. Usually, they are rather innocuous, though, and don't tend to cause too much of a problem. Still, their presence should be a clear indication that something larger is lurking nearby.

Frightening Inhuman Apparitions

The whole purpose of negative entities is to feed on fear, which means they are very good at being scary. Like most predators, they've evolved certain qualities to assist in this feeding process. These entities will often have a terrifying appearance that includes things like sharp needle teeth, large red or yellow eyes, scaly skin, wings like a bat, devilish horns, or worse. It's important to remember that these entities don't have physical bodies, so these apparitions are just projections used to produce the desired fear meal they are seeking. While human spirits and poltergeists can create all kinds of weird activity, it's nearly unheard of for them to present themselves as terrifying creatures.

Scratching and Biting

While many types of spirits are capable of physical contact, negative entities have a special affinity for scratching and biting, whereas human spirits will often go for shoving, poking, or hitting. When afflicted by a scratch from a negative entity, most folks describe feeling a burning sensation followed by a reddening of the skin, and then the scratch marks appear. This generally happens in a matter of moments.

Nightmares

Those afflicted with a negative-entity haunting will often suffer from nightmares. There are two possible explanations for this, the first being that the entity may cause the nightmares in order to stir up more fear. Alternatively, it's often believed that our subconscious picks up on the presence of these entities long before our conscious mind does and will therefore try to warn us through nightmares.

Sleep Paralysis

Sleep paralysis is an extremely frightening phenomenon that occurs when the mind wakes up while the body stays asleep. Folks awake to find themselves completely paralyzed, unable to move or speak. Unfortunately, it often gets worse. Those suffering from a sudden bout of sleep paralysis often describe an intense psychic awareness, such as being able to see the room very clearly even though their eyes are closed. Other times, they may become aware of a spirit presence in the room, and it's usually unfriendly. The sheer terror that often accompanies sleep paralysis creates a lot of energy for negative entities to feed off, and even when the home is not occupied by an entity, these events can sort of chum the water and draw them in. Of course, there are scientific explanations for sleep paralysis; however, if the affected person has no history of sleep paralysis until moving into the haunted home, the reason could be supernatural in nature. Sometimes I suspect the paralysis is caused directly by the entity in order to feed, especially in the case of phenomena like hag riding, which is a form of sleep paralysis that is accompanied by a spirit sitting on the chest of the victim.

Agreements

Through my interactions with these beings, my own research, and my conversations with other professionals, I have come to understand that inhuman spirits have to play by certain rules. Chief among them is that they have to have our permission in order to interact with us. This idea is something that is found throughout a great deal of folklore concerning meddling spirits. But how does this work out in real life? How come they haunt homes and bully people every day despite this cosmic law? Let's take it point by point:

1: Negative entities and other inhuman spirits are not allowed to interact with or harm you *unless they have your permission.*

2: Making agreements and giving permission is much easier than you would think. You can do so with your emotions, your thoughts, and your beliefs. For instance, if you are thinking and believing that the entity can hurt you, then you are agreeing that it has that ability and thus giving it permission. However, if you are not afraid and know it can't hurt you, it won't be able to. Even so, it will try to do things like move objects near you in order to get you to second-guess and make an agreement. When I teach this work, I begin this section by asking for a show of hands from the class if they've heard of a situation in which a knife or other dangerous object was thrown across a room by a spirit. Most of the class routinely raise their hands. I then ask them to keep their hands raised if the object hit a person, causing them injury or death. Never have I ever had a hand remain raised. This is because while the entity doesn't have permission to hurt you, it can cut it *really* close to get your reaction—like the worst game of "I'm not touching you" ever. A lot of the time, if the spirit gets close, it gets the person to believe that it can hurt them, and thus the person gives it permission.

3: Agreements are why the vast majority of hauntings start slowly, with whispers or knocking on walls. After a bit, people usually start to knock back. That's an invitation and an agreement that the entity is allowed to interact with you. This is why Ouija boards and certain forms of divination used to contact the dead or anything across the veil are dangerous. You can make a lot of agreements very quickly without realizing it.

4: Fear is an agreement. Not only does fear feed the entity (more on that later) and make it stronger, but it also creates an agreement. If you're afraid that the entity will hurt you, then you believe it can, and it will use that as permission. This doesn't mean you will never be afraid or nervous in a paranormal situation—I've nearly peed my pants on several occasions. Just do your best not to let that fear control you. As long as you remain in control, you still call the shots.

5: Entities will target children to get agreements from their parents. First of all, children are really easy to make agreements with. The entity shows up as an imaginary friend and is invited to a tea party, and before they know it, the child is up to their eyeballs in agreements. When parents are faced with their child being harassed by an entity, the first thing out of their mouths usually is, "Come after me instead." *Boom!* Agreement City! This is usually the entity's intention all along: to build the agreements with the child and then transfer them over to a parent.

6: Breaking agreements is easy: simply state out loud that you no longer agree, and mean it. You can revoke permission and break agreements at any time, as long as you do so confidently and without fear. If you are afraid or you believe that it won't work, then it won't, because you are continuing to agree that the entity doesn't have to listen to you. A statement such as, "I break any and all agreements with this entity, and it is no longer welcome to be near me or interact with me," is usually plenty. This doesn't mean the entity just flies off into the ether, never to be seen again. But it does get it to step back and lose a good deal of its power. Without this, it has a "Get Out of Exorcism Free" card. Also, parents can speak on their children's behalf and break agreements that they have made. This leads me to my next point...

7: It's not necessarily that the entity needs your permission to interact with you specifically; it simply needs permission from a human to interact with another human, which is why you can break agreements on behalf of your children and also why people can agree to allow a spirit to hurt another person. As long as a living person gives it permission, it is allowed.

8: Agreements don't always look or seem like agreements. Some hauntings start with a knock at the door, and when you open the door, no one is there. It's possible that this is a spirit asking to enter your home, and by opening the door, you agree to it.

9: Once negative entities are removed from the home (exorcised), they will quickly attempt to make agreements that allow them to return. Similarly, during an exorcism they'll often make a ruckus in order to get you to believe—and therefore agree—that it's not working so that they don't have to leave.

10: Dwelling on the memories of the haunting, or obsessively fearing the return of the haunting, can be used as an agreement to return. That's why when I leave a home, I tell folks to move on like it never happened. When folks immediately begin talking about it, reliving the experience, and getting afraid or worked up, they inadvertently call the entity back in.

11: Positive entities (angels, guardians, beings of light, and so on) are similarly bound. You have to give them permission to protect you in the same manner that negative things need your permission to harm you. So, making agreements with benevolent, protective spirits is helpful in this work.

12: Human ghosts don't seem to be quite as bound by this rule as inhuman entities are. This means they have a little more wiggle room when it comes to interacting with people. We still have the ability to restrict them from certain things through force of will.

For instance, a ghost doesn't need your permission to influence you, but if you tell them that they're not allowed to influence you, they won't be able to, or at least it will be a lot more difficult. There is nuance to this, but we each have a say in what is allowed in our energetic field.

The Boggart Effect

By now we understand that negative entities feed on fear. Furthermore, fear weakens us and makes us much more susceptible to making agreements with them. In a sense, when we are afraid, we get much smaller while they get a lot bigger. Therefore, finding ways to not be afraid is paramount. When teaching folks how to do this, I often find myself talking about the boggart creatures from the Harry Potter series, because negative entities function in the same way. They know what scares you and will use it against you. However, if you can find a way to make it comical, then you have a huge advantage. They hate laughter, and laughing at them tends to wound them in a way. I often find that if I visualize a huge pink Kentucky Derby hat on just about any entity, it ceases to be very frightening. Similarly, naming a big, scary entity "Bob" or "Fred" really helps take the scare factor down a few notches.

When it comes to interacting with the negative entity, I often try to do so with the energy of a parent speaking to an unruly child. You must be firm and let it know how things are going to be. If it acts up and throws things, you'll need to remain patient but otherwise unfazed. I find that if I can't muster up something funny, simply remaining bored or unimpressed often does the trick. It wants a reaction out of you, and remaining stony robs it of its fear meal and its ability to make an agreement that it can harm you.

While negative entities can be dangerous, you'll come to find that they are big softies once you stop being afraid of them.

The Nest

Though every haunting is unique, I've found that most household negative entities follow a pattern, one of which is setting up shop in one particular location. I call this the "nest." It's from here that the entity roots into the home and begins to spread outward. It's also here that it will retreat to rest and recuperate when it's not causing activity in the home. Identifying where the nest is, as well as locations that may potentially become nesting ground, is crucial to this work.

Habitat

While you can find a nest just about anywhere, my experience has taught me that there are certain types of rooms and conditions that make for perfect nesting habitat. The first thing that makes a good nesting ground is a space that is often undisturbed. This means that places like the guest bedroom you haven't gone into in months, the storage closet in the basement where you keep your Christmas decorations, and the cupboard under the stairs all make excellent spaces for an entity to make a nest.

The second thing that makes good nesting ground is stagnant energy. This is part of the reason why entities look for places that are undisturbed. When we open spaces up and move things around, we are moving energy and freshening the space. Places that are cluttered or don't receive much sunlight or activity tend to be full of stagnant energy. This is also why basements tend to be ideal nesting ground as well: because the energy settles downward and then stagnates. This thick, unmoving energy becomes like molasses, and the entity can squish down into it. And once it does, it's much harder to remove. It's a bit like a tree that gets its roots down into the soil.

Identifying the Nest

At this point in my classes, a hand usually goes up to ask, "How will we know when we've found the nest?" My answer is always, *"You will know."* It's the place where, when you come across it, your hair stands up. It's the room that you open the door to and immediately say, "I don't like how this feels." It's a very distinct feeling of negativity, to the point that it makes some folks nauseated. Many folks experience feeling fear when entering these spaces, or a feeling of trespassing or being stalked by a predator. I suppose it's the same feeling that ancient humans developed to let them know that the cave they went into for shelter was also home to a saber-toothed tiger lurking deep inside, watching them from the shadows. If you have concerns that you won't be able to identify the nest, you can always lean on your pendulum to confirm if you've found the right location. Also, entities do not like it when you identify the location and will occasionally act out and do things like slam the door in your face or otherwise try to keep you out. If something like that does happen, you'll know for certain you've found the right place. In other cases, the space may seem darker than it should be, as if it were eating the light. Also, perfectly ordinary objects in a room, such as pieces of art or stuffed animals, may take on an oddly sinister energy. When you find the nest, *you will know*.

If, for some reason, you have strong reason to believe that a negative entity is present but you are not finding anything that seems like a nest, it may mean a few things. First, it could mean that the haunting is new and the entity hasn't had enough time to really root down anywhere. The process takes time. If you can confirm that the haunting is in fact new, this is good news. The entity isn't anchored, so it will be much easier to remove. You'll just have to cleanse the house really well. Second, sometimes the whole house feels like a nest; that happens when the entity has had a lot of time to get comfy and spread throughout the home. An initial cleansing of the space may uncover its location. Third, the entity may be anchored to a person instead of a place. We'll talk about that a little later. Fourth, sometimes they live in places like a mirror or are anchored to an object. These are things you'll be able to figure out by interviewing the client and doing your investigative work. In most cases, though, you will be dealing with an entity that exhibits nesting behavior.

The Importance of the Nest

Identifying the nest is paramount for entity removal. This is the place where the entity has anchored itself into the home, meaning this is its point of attachment and where it is most vulnerable. It is here where the bulk of your exorcism will take place and where you will want to focus your efforts the most. You can cleanse the rest of the home until you are blue in the face, but the entity will stay anchored from the nest and will easily resist exorcism. We must go into the entity's home and deal with it there if we are to be successful.

The Spreading Infection

Once the entity has entered the home and established its nest, it will then begin to spread throughout the home like an infection. It does this through lowering the vibration of the home by spreading fear, exhaustion, and sadness while simultaneously making agreements with the human inhabitants. Negative entities that haven't had much time to get settled will often be very weak. An entity that has been given enough time, however, will spread its roots from the nest all throughout the house, staking its claim. The longer the haunting goes on, the harder the entity will be to remove. No worries, it can still be done—it just takes more time. I often feel this infection growing in the walls, floors, and ceilings. In my mind, I get the sense that if I were to punch a hole in the wall and look in, I would find roots snaking through like veins, all coming from the nest. The whole home itself may feel unusually dark or unwelcoming when the infection has taken hold. An early-stage house will feel very different from a late-stage house.

The Removal Process

The process of exorcising a space is simple in theory; you simply raise the vibration until the space becomes uninhabitable to the entity and it is forced to vacate the premises. Think of it like the energetic equivalent to producing a high-pitched sound that they hate and drives them out. To accomplish this, you'll need to cleanse the space of stale or dark negative energy and then invite in higher holy powers. Giving the space up to a higher power—"God," "Goddess," the "Divine," and so on—often creates the biggest shift and is the most helpful in removing the entity.

Now, some of you are probably wondering, "If I'm a witch, why would I rely on the Divine? Why don't I just do it myself with my own will and power?" The answer is that bringing in the higher power bypasses the need for you to have direct confrontation with the entity itself. Sometimes, in the early stages of an entity haunting, you may be able to just magic it out of the home. Other times, going head-to-head with certain entities will not end well for you, no matter how powerful of a witch you think you are. Giving the space to a higher power doesn't mean that the space is then a temple to them; it simply means you are placing the problem in their hands. This combination of cleansing and inviting in beneficial energy is the one-two punch that makes this process work safely.

Below we will discuss the steps you may need to take to achieve this. These steps are listed in order, and I suggest following this sequence. For this section, we will be assuming that you've already done your walk-throughs, identified the type(s) of haunting, and found the nest. If you have not yet done all of that, please go back and start from the beginning.

Prework

This step may or may not be necessary, depending on the severity of the haunting. If it's relatively new and the entity is weak and just making a closet or cupboard feel strange, you can probably skip to the next step. If, however, the haunting has been allowed to go on for a while and the infection has spread throughout the house, or you suspect more than one type of haunting is present, you will definitely need to do the prework.

This step consists of doing an initial cleansing of the home. Whether you choose to use smoke, water, or sound—or a combination—is up to you. This step is important, because it takes care of a few issues. First, if the infection has had time to spread, this helps to ease its grip on the home, thus making the entity easier to banish. Second, sometimes you may suspect there is a negative entity but may be having trouble judging where one haunting ends and another begins. Other times, the whole house feels weird, which can make it difficult to determine the location of the nest. Doing an initial surface scrub can help get rid of the psychic static and help you determine where the problem areas are. Third, this will give you an opportunity to move any lingering earthbound human spirits through the light and address any portals (see chapter 12). If the entity is new or otherwise not securely attached to the home yet, it may flee at this point. However, one that's had time to settle in will resist banishment during this first indirect pass.

When faced with a home that is deeply infected by an entity, I find it helpful to focus specifically on the walls and floors of the home, because the energy anchoring the entity is often embedded in these areas. To do so, I like to use my intention and place my hand on a wall and push with my mind and my energy. In my experience, this causes a puff of dark energy to be released from the wall, a little like when you smack a dusty cushion and a cloud of particles gets released. I see this in my mind's eye like black smoke being expelled. I prefer to do this when I'm cleansing with a bowl of salt water, and I find that placing a wet, salty hand on the wall really gives this some extra oomph. The black drawing candles (see pages 34 and 189) also come in handy during this process, as they give you somewhere to send the negative energy once it's released. These candles also draw the bad energy out of the walls on their own, making your job easier. This process is like sucking the poison out of the home, and as the negative energy is removed, the entity's grip on the home loosens. During this process, you will start to feel the energy of the home shift; it may feel lighter, brighter, or simply like you can breathe more easily. Most of this work is done through feel, so stay in touch with this sense as you go.

When cleansing, I normally follow a heating and cooling cycle by first using smoke (heating) and then sprinkling water (cooling). However, when it comes to dealing with a deeply infected home, I will do the opposite and start with the water, as well as the wall presses, and then follow that with smoke cleansing to clean up and make sure any darkness expelled from the walls doesn't linger.

The Exorcism

Next comes the intense part: removing the entity from the nest. While you do need to be careful and take precautions, I've rarely had an issue besides it being stubborn. It may make a racket with flickering lights or slamming doors, but the key is to not let yourself be rattled by it. I recommend coming at these spirits with a rather bored energy. After some time, and a few exorcisms, you get used to the old song and dance anyway. Any activity that kicks up around you during the process is simply the entity trying to get you to believe that what you are doing is not working. Remain calm, focused, and matter-of-fact. It's going to leave, because it has no other choice. It can be mad, but it still has to go. Now is also probably a good time to inform you of my favorite personal motto: "'Paranormal investigation' starts with P(ee)." This means it's best to start every investigation (and exorcism) with a trip to the little investigator's room. That way, if something happens that startles you, you don't have an oopsie. Moving on…

The exorcism takes place in the nesting area. Do not attempt an exorcism at night; I recommend always doing these during the day and giving yourself a couple of hours to get the job done. Before you go in, make sure that you are grounded and heavily protected (see chapter 1) and that you have everything you need with you. When you enter the nesting area, tell the entity that it is no longer welcome and it's time for it to leave. *Do not engage with the entity beyond telling it that it needs to get out*, which you can repeat throughout the process. Don't have any sort of conversation with it, and resist the urge to antagonize it, provoke it, or challenge it to a fight. These are all agreements. Keep your statements short and straightforward. This is not a discussion. It needs to leave, end of story.

◆———————◆

Ritual

PERFORMING AN EXORCISM

Remember, *we are removing the entity by cleansing the area, raising the vibration, and giving the space to a higher power.* As you do this, you'll want to treat the whole room, but you should focus mainly on the precise area of the room where you feel the entity is squatting. So, for instance, if you find an entity in the back corner of the guest bedroom, you'll want to work on the whole guest bedroom but focus mainly on that back corner. Your job is to make the space unlivable for the entity through cleansing, while also telling it to leave and asking for assistance from your higher power.

I begin by lighting a white candle to represent the light I am bringing into the room and saying a prayer that invites my benevolent higher power into the space. I then pick up my bowl of cleansing water (see chapter 2) and declare that the entity needs to leave. I then use the cleansing water with strong will and intention and sprinkle it about the room while asking that the negativity and toxic energy of the entity be lifted and removed. This helps to establish you and your higher power's ownership of the space. After treating the room itself, I focus my cleansing efforts in the precise area in which I feel the entity is squatting. I spend extra time there, and I pray profusely that the entity's unwelcome presence be lifted out of the space and banished from the home, while sprinkling the cleansing water with strong will and intention.

Once I feel the room start to lighten, I then light incense like frankincense, a purification herb like juniper or rosemary, or camphor and take the smoke around the room in a counterclockwise fashion, making sure to waft it into all corners as well as under beds and tables. Again, once that's done, I return to face the entity. At this time I often like to set the smoking incense down right where I feel the entity is and begin to pray. I aim for a balance between telling the entity to leave and inviting in the benevolent higher power to remove it. Remember to stay calm and focused. If you'd like to incorporate sound by clapping, ringing bells, or striking chimes, now would be the time to do it. Some entities may be stubborn, but don't give up. Keep going, and really *feel* the process working. Will it to happen. Visualize it happening. And most importantly, *let it happen.* Don't worry about when or if it will happen; trust that it *is* happening.

During the exorcism process, you may add other steps as you feel necessary. You may open the windows in the space to bring in fresh air that helps to lift the energy. You may draw holy or protective symbols on the walls with special oils. This is a bit like planting a flag on the space and claiming ownership of it in the name of your higher power. You may use a holy anointing oil from a church or a condition oil like Cast Off Evil oil, Blessing oil, or any type of purifying or blessing oil you prefer. In a pinch, use essential oils like rosemary, camphor, or eucalyptus diluted in olive oil. I also like to finish up by sprinkling blessed salt (see page 192) in all the corners—but be sure not to finish up until you feel the entity is gone.

You're probably wondering, "How will I know when it's gone?" and my unhelpful answer is, *You will know*. It's an unmistakable feeling. Suddenly something lifts, and the whole room feels different. It seems lighter and brighter; it may even sound clearer, or you may be able to breathe more easily. When I bring the family back into the space, they often remark on how different it feels as well. You need to keep up this cleansing and vibrational lifting process until you feel this shift take place. It may begin to feel better, but wait until you absolutely feel the entity exit. These things take time, so please have patience, be thorough, and don't try to rush the process.

Troubleshooting

If the entity has had a lot of time to dig itself into the energy of the home, you may have to do prework in the nest area *before* going into the exorcism. Do this first, before anything else. Light a black drawing candle and go around pushing on the walls, as discussed above, to pull out the bad energy and send it to the candle. This will help loosen the entity's grip so that it's easier to remove.

Don't be afraid to work with other forms of cleansing. If the water cleansing I've described above doesn't speak to you, try a fire cleansing or something else. I often get asked, "Should I try _____ cleansing?" and the answer is always, "Couldn't hurt, might help!" So if you want to approach this with a different method of cleansing that feels stronger in your hands, please feel free to go back to the material in chapter 2 on cleansing and pick the one you like better. Sometimes different entities react better to different types of cleansing, so don't be afraid to experiment or go a different route if you are making no headway. Also, don't forget to change your own energy as well: take a big, deep breath and slowly exhale, letting go of your own tension and letting the negative energy go as you cleanse.

Lastly, if you are having trouble with the whole "higher power" thing, simplify it. The Divine is a huge concept to try to wrap your head around. If that's not working for you, there are alternatives, such as inviting in "light" or "gratitude" or "blessings" or "love" instead of a deity or higher power. You can also call in compassion, mercy, and understanding. Similarly, if you like an animistic approach, you can show love and gratitude to the room. Each of these things has power, so if you aren't down with the Divine, call in something that makes your heart feel good.

Remember to have strong, clear intention and to really do the process like you mean business. No entity is gonna respect you if you go in there and half-heartedly mutter, "Please leave."

Afterwork

Once the entity is gone and you feel the dramatic shift in the nesting area, you're mostly done with the exorcism. However, sometimes the entity isn't really gone; it's simply wounded and hiding somewhere else in the house. Since it's weak and has no anchor point to secure its presence in the home, it can be easily sent away. Simply going over the home from top to bottom one more time with cleansing incense is generally enough to make sure nothing else is lingering. Be sure to waft some of the smoke into attics and crawl spaces.

Once you've done your final cleanse, you must then secure the space to make sure the entity doesn't come back. At the very least, you'll need to go and mark the doorways and windowsills with protective symbols using a special oil, such as Fiery Wall of Protection, or a brew of protective herbs, such as rue, basil, or angelica. You'll find some helpful spells for this in chapter 11.

The Attached Entity

Many folks ask me, "How do I know if I have an attached negative entity?" and my unhelpful answer yet again is, *You will know*. Still, folks can be oddly blind to the reality. These folks frequently send me messages along the lines of, "I've been haunted by an entity for the better part of twenty-two years. It's with me wherever I go, and I have repeated dreams that it's attached to me via a black cord sticking out of my back. How do I know if I have an entity attachment?" At this point, I usually resist the urge to bang my head against the table. While we need to take into consideration things like psychological and neurological issues and must avoid jumping to conclusions, if it walks like a duck and talks like a duck, it's probably a duck.

Things to look for when diagnosing this issue include dreams of something being attached to the person or a feeling of being "ridden" or like something is on their back or just behind them all the time. Also, entities that follow a person from place to place are often attached to the host. Many folks with entity attachments will claim to have had them for years, sometimes decades. This leads to people being oddly fond of the entity, even if it torments them incessantly. Their emotional attachment to the entity can prove to be an issue, and after it's removed, they may feel lonely and wish for it to return, thus forming an agreement allowing it to come back.

When working with an entity that is attached to a person, you must be careful. It can act out and try to harm you or the client during the process. Please get some magical and paranormal experience under your belt before attempting to remove a negative entity from a person, and be sure to have all your protections in place. If in doubt, reach out to a more experienced professional for assistance. Below I will walk you through some of the finer points of the process, and then we'll dive into the removal technique.

Why Do Entities Attach to Humans?

In my experience, they often attach in order to feed off the host's energy—usually their fear, their sexual energy, or their life force. Due to this last source, folks with an attached entity will feel drained, and they may even become seriously ill. Many will seek medical help, but doctors will come up with nothing. Entities may influence our thoughts and emotions much like earthbound human spirits, and attaching to the host makes this process much easier. Living in the city, I saw many homeless folks with addiction issues and debilitating mental health concerns who would walk around with an entity floating along behind them silently, like a shadow, with its hand stuck through the back of their head, driving them further into their addictions and worsening their mental state. These folks are often easy targets for sinister spiritual forces. Other times the entity will use the human host as an anchor, sort of like a nest. If they are attached to a host, they can't be banished. From what I can tell, the ones that attach to people and the ones that attach to homes are two separate species of entity. Similarly, those that seek to attach to people and those that seek to *possess* people are also different.

Where Do Entities Attach?

Negative entities will usually attach at four specific places. Most commonly, they will attach at the back of the neck or between the shoulder blades. I've also seen them attach at the base of the spine and through the solar plexus, but those are less common. I suspect attached entities may "plug in" at just about any energy center, but these main four seem to be the favorites.

How Do Entities Become Attached?

Through an agreement with the host, of course. Remember, all inhuman entities require our permission to interact with us, let alone attach to us. This doesn't always mean the permission was intentional, but in some way we did let it happen. Taking responsibility for allowing an entity to attach to us is the first step to removing it. This realization helps us to prevent it happening again in the future and gives us the power to break the agreement. Remember, all it takes is a simple declaration to break the agreement. Removing the entity, though, is another story.

How Is a Negative-Entity Attachment Different?

There are many spirits that will seek to invade our bodies, and folks sometimes have difficulty separating an attached negative entity from an astral parasite or a possession by a demon or nature spirit. While they all include invasion and influence on the host, they are vastly different. For instance, an astral parasite is like a leech or a tick. They may attach to us all over our body and slowly feed on our energy.

On the other hand, demonic entities may seek to completely take over a body through possession. They also tend to have heavy religious overtones and will either fear or seek to destroy things like Christian icons and statues. While negative entities can be removed by invoking the name of God, they don't usually have beef with Christianity. And while they may, in short bursts, possess and control the host, they do so only when forced and don't seek to take over the body long-term. They just like to hook themselves to the host and use them as a battery, occasionally squeezing more juice out of the person by attacking them physically or emotionally by changing their moods or introducing harsh negative thought patterns.

Removing the Attached Entity

I'm going to walk you through the method that I use, but first I want to help you get to know the moving parts so that you know why I do what I do. If you don't understand the "why," you'll never be able to adapt it as needed.

The first thing you'll need to do is to identify where the entity is attached to the person. Usually, the person will have some idea, based on where they can feel it in their body or what visuals (such as dreams) they've received during their time with the entity. If you aren't sure, you can ask a pendulum, or if you reach your hand out, you'll be able to feel the attachment if your energy-sensing skills are up to the job. I recommend using a combination of the above to locate precisely where the entity is attached, as knowing this is essential to the process. Remember, when sensing the location yourself, don't invite it in, and stay heavily protected when anywhere near the entity.

Once you've found it, you'll need something to loosen the attachment. When an entity plugs into a person, it grows roots. Just severing the cord will leave this root in, and that can cause problems later on, sort of like when you pull a tick off of you but leave the head attached. Using a substance to loosen it or pull it to the surface, where it can be cleared more easily, can make all the difference.

Second, you will need something to clear or sever the attachment. You may use something as simple as a kitchen knife. In my experience, it also helps to bless the knife with a prayer and a sprinkle of holy water or an anointing oil. If you or your client are not comfortable with using an actual knife, you have some alternatives. I purchased a stick of selenite that is roughly the size and shape of a knife, and it works rather well. In Mexican culture, we often use lemons to clear negative attachments as well. Sounds unorthodox, I know, but sour things like citrus fruits have a very sharp cutting energy. I use lemons in relationship cord-cutting rituals all the time, and though I've never used one for this exact procedure, in theory it should work the same. Simply cleanse it, say a prayer or a blessing over it, glide it across the host's skin where the entity is connected, and it should slice right through. You may also call upon powerful spirit helpers like Saint Michael, who can use his sword to help you cut through the cord, or Hekate, who can do the same with her knife.

Third, you'll want something to absorb and trap the entity. I like to use a black candle, because it's something I often have on hand in my "work" bag. I suppose you could use a crystal like clear quartz, but I've honestly never tried it. I like the naturally absorbent qualities that come with a black candle, since black, being a void-like color that eats other colors, lends a very hungry energy to it. Plus, the fact that it's a candle allows it to be burned with the entity inside it, making it a versatile tool. More on that later.

Please do not attempt this on anyone who has shown violent tendencies related to the influence of the spirit attachment. The entity may use the host to try to fight you off. You don't need someone punching you in the nose halfway through the removal because the entity wants to stay. Either way, it's best to have another person in the room in case the spirit tries to act out through the client.

Ritual

THE REMOVAL OF AN ATTACHED ENTITY

Here I will show you how I prefer to do the removal. Please only attempt this with your protections in place and adequate magical experience under your belt. This process can be dangerous. Remain calm. Stay focused.

Before you begin, have a conversation with the client. Make sure they are ready to be free of the entity. You'll be surprised at how common it is for folks to want to keep the entity. Usually, it's been with them so long that they aren't sure what life looks like without it. If they are serious and ready to be free of it, they will have to say so. They need to speak the words out loud and without fear. They have to mean it. The statement should be something to the effect of, "I break all agreements with this entity. It is no longer welcome in my life, and I free myself from it now and forever." Once they speak the words, you may continue. Let them know before you start that the process may be uncomfortable. Some people experience pain or panic during the removal. Others don't feel a thing. As long as you and the client are safe, continue through the discomfort.

To start, you'll want to locate the attachment. If you're using a pendulum for this, I would not hold it over the client's body, as the entity may interfere with it. I would do this in another room and use a piece of paper with a drawing of a body on it to divine where the attachment is located. Once you have a sense for where it is attached, you can go in and see if you can feel it. Don't be too open around the entity, but a little energy sensing won't cause you any problems. You may feel the wispy strings of the attachment or feel an unnaturally cold energy. Once you've identified the location, you can move on to step two.

Step two is the prep stage. It's here when you will want to use something to loosen or draw out the attachment. I like to use my special Cut and Clear oil for this (see page 209). It's not strong enough to sever an attachment like this, but it does a good job of bringing it to the surface, where it's easier to remove. Simply apply it by hand over the area of attachment. Don't be afraid to really grease it up and cover more skin than you think you may need. Just, you know, don't be creepy.

Step three is the removal itself. Take the black candle in your dominant hand. I like to use your standard black stick candle. You may choose to use a black novena candle as well, but that is a long burn time to have something like that hanging around in the house. Conversely, I wouldn't use something too small like a chime candle or a birthday candle. A sturdy stick candle or a small pillar candle will be perfect. Just be sure to cleanse it first. You'll also want a clear mental picture of what an entity looks like. To me, it generally looks like a humanoid shadow, attached to the host by a black cord. Just understanding how this looks in general terms will help you do the work. You don't have to have a highly accurate image in mind—just a general image will do. Do *not* spend any time looking at the entity, though. Do not engage with the entity, and do not talk to it or look at it for any meaningful amount of time. Ignore it. Hold the candle in your dominant hand and your cutting tool in the other. Make sure you're properly grounded and centered. To begin, activate the candle with a mental command, using strong will and intention. For me, it's a bit like turning on a super-powered hand vacuum. If you're doing it correctly, you may feel it catch as the entity begins to get sucked up. Once the entity starts to get sucked into the candle, increase the drawing power. To me, this feels energetically a bit like reeling in a fish. I recommend pulling the candle back just a little as you go, to keep the tension as the rest of the entity and the cord get drawn in. This usually happens quickly, and you can sense when it disappears into the candle. Do not lose focus.

Once the entity has been drawn into the candle, it will still be attached to the person by the cord, which at this point will be pulled tight between the person and the candle with the entity inside. Once you've reached this stage, keep the tension on the cord by keeping the suction on high and pulling back just an inch or two with the candle. The tension is important for the next part. In one smooth motion—and with strong will and intention—cut upward through the cord using the cutting tool. I prefer to cut upward, as it's a much more freeing and releasing gesture to go up and out in an arc as opposed to cutting downward, which is a closing and gathering motion. Since you have good tension on the cord, the cut should be clean and the slack should snap right into the candle. Voilà, the entity is released from the person and trapped in the candle. However, we are not done yet. Keep the candle active and pass it over the area where the entity was attached to pull out any bits or roots left in the person. Once you feel it's all drawn out, pull the candle back and lock the entity inside with a mental command that the candle is closed. If the entity is rather rowdy, you may wrap red or white string around the candle three times and tie it with three knots to keep it contained while you tend to the client.

Aftercare

Now is when you need to check in with the client and make sure they are okay. I've never had someone be traumatized or injured, but sometimes they can become emotional as they feel the release. Extending compassion to your client is essential. Once you've done that, you have some energetic first aid to do. At this point, they have a massive energetic crater that needs to be healed. If you are trained in a modality such as Reiki, you can use those skills to send healing energy to the area until you feel it fill and relax. If you are not Reiki trained, I recommend holding your hands together and visualizing a ball of beautiful, soft golden light forming there and growing until it's about the size of a grapefruit; then, gently place it into the hole left by the entity and see the light melt, filling and healing the space.

Once that is done, I smoke the client down with some cleansing incense and send them to immediately take a spiritual bath. The bath I usually prescribe is a fifty-fifty mix of sea salt and Epsom salts as well as cleansing plants like hyssop or lime juice. This just helps to clear away any lingering bits or pieces of attachment. I ask them to soak for about ten to twenty minutes, making sure to fully immerse at least once. When taking a spiritual bath, it's important to open yourself up to the plants and salts and let them do their job of scrubbing you. When the client is done, I recommend that they air-dry, anoint themselves with protective oils, and then get in bed and rest. I suggest you take the same bath when you get done with this work.

While the client is having the bath, I recommend smoke cleansing the home to get rid of anything that may be lingering, as well as setting up protections against the return of the entity.

Ritual

THE BANISHMENT OF
AN ATTACHED ENTITY

The next thing I recommend doing is a banishing ritual to dispose of the candle and the entity trapped inside.

You'll need sewing pins, black peppercorns, a plate, a mortar and pestle, and banishing oil.

Take the candle and dress it with the banishing oil, saying prayers or incantations requesting that the entity be sent far away, never to return. Next, insert three, five, or nine sewing pins into the candle to weaken the entity. Gently heat the bottom of the candle and affix it to the plate. Crush the black peppercorns in a mortar and pestle while saying prayers or incantations of banishment, and then encircle the candle counterclockwise with the crushed pepper. Light the candle and visualize with strong will that the entity in the candle gets blasted out like a bullet streaking far away from you. I often see it going farther and farther until it shoots past the end of the earth and out into space, where it drifts off into the abyss. Set the intention that every second the candle burns, the entity is pushed farther and farther away. Let the candle burn all the way down, scrape any leftover wax into a baggie with some salt, and throw it in a dumpster far away from your home. When you're done, go take a cleansing bath with salt, hyssop, and lemons or lemon juice.

Object Attachments and Conduits

Sometimes negative entities and evil spirits will attach themselves to items instead of people or places. These items are often referred to as "conduits" and are essentially puppets used by entities to interact with our world. These are often dolls and toys, but they can be just about anything from sports memorabilia and cars to mirrors and even television sets. While some of these may be cleansed, others will have to be thrown in the trash or given to a professional to watch over. I don't suggest donating them to a thrift store, because that's just mean.

If for some reason the conduit returns, you may need to perform a binding on the object. I recommend wrapping the object three times with sturdy white or red cord and then knotting it three times. If the object is a doll, I would blindfold it and tie its hands and feet as well.

The trick is that you have to remember that the doll is being used as a proxy and isn't the actual spirit. However, this is a two-way street: the same way the entity affects the object, we can use the object to affect the entity. We call this sympathetic magic, in which we use a representation of something or someone and work magic on it to affect them. Without the understanding that we are exploiting this connection, the work will likely fall flat. So, keep in mind that by binding the object you are also, through the object, binding the spirit.

If you would like to take it a step further, you may dismantle the object and then bury it and bless the ground where it is buried. This should neutralize the entity's ability to use it as a conduit. Be sure to do your follow-up cleansing of the home it inhabited and place protections as usual.

Client Homework

Once the entity has been removed, how the clients proceed can make or break the entire process. With the wrong attitude or habits, they may invite the spirit right back in as soon as you leave. My general rules can be found at the end of chapter 5, but it all boils down to this: the client must try to move on from the haunting as if it never happened. Dwelling on the activity or living in fear that it will return at any moment will only invite it back in. I also recommend putting the family on a cleansing schedule that they do themselves after you leave. I often prescribe daily cleansing for a week, then once a week for a month or two after that, and then once a month from then on out. This will help keep anything from returning and will give the client some of their power back.

CHAPTER 11

Your Magical Toolkit

This chapter serves as a grimoire of helpful rituals, recipes, and techniques that you may find useful when working against negative and inhuman entities. Many of these are ones that I've developed myself, so they may have a Christian folk-magic flair, but all of them are adaptable to your unique needs. These have served me well, and I now pass them on to you.

Candle Rituals

Below you will find two of my favorite rituals for turning common candles into weapons for your spiritual arsenal. Remember to always practice fire safety when working with these.

Ritual

DARK MOON BLACK DRAWING CANDLES

You can make a black drawing candle on the fly the way I described on page 34. However, it can be handy to have some supercharged ones ready to go. This is the ritual I use to bless and consecrate these nifty tools on the dark moon.

You'll need black stick candles, a carving tool, dark moon water, dragon's blood incense, and a black cloth.

On the night of the dark moon (when it's completely black), set out the above tools in low candlelight. Light the incense and waft the candles through the smoke to cleanse them. Using a carving tool like a nail or a needle, you may inscribe symbols into the wax. These can be simple, such as a clockwise spiral starting from the outside and working your way in to symbolize the energy being drawn into the candles, or you can get fancy and use sigils or other symbols of power that match this purpose. Once you are done, sprinkle all of the candles with dark moon water (water that has been left out under the dark moon). As you do this, speak some prayers or words of power over them and visualize that they all become sucking black holes. Hold this image until you feel them activate. Once you do, wrap them in the black cloth to keep them from sucking up anything and everything until you're ready to use them. Later, before you use them, tap them three times on a table or surface to wake them up.

Ritual

WHITE LIGHT CANDLES

While black is a highly absorbent color, white is very projective. It can fill a space with protection and healing as well as help bring in and sustain the presence of helpful spirit entities. This ritual is for the blessing and consecration of "white light" candles. These are helpful for restoring good energy to a room after a heavy cleansing. I often light one of these in the home last or leave one or two with the family to light themselves after I'm gone, as an act of beginning again.

You'll need white candles, a carving tool, holy water, frankincense incense, and a white cloth.

On a Sunday morning, find a patch of beautiful sunlight and set out your tools. Light the incense and waft the candles through the smoke to cleanse them. Using a carving tool like a nail or a needle, you may inscribe symbols into the wax. These can be simple, such as a cross, or you can get fancy and use sigils, runes, or other symbols of holy power that you wish to. Once you are done, sprinkle all of the candles with holy water. As you do this, speak some prayers (particularly the Our Father, Hail Mary, or Psalm 23) or words of power over them and visualize them collecting the sunlight until they are bursting with beautiful white light. Once you feel them activate, wrap them up in white cloth to protect them and keep them charged until you need them. When you're ready to use them, tap these three times on a table or surface to wake them up, and light them in any space to fill it with light and shift the energy in a positive direction.

Blessed Items

Below I'll be talking you through the process of blessing certain substances, such as salt and water. These are excellent to make ahead of time and then pack into a kit for use in the field. The act of blessing further programs and empowers them so that they become more than just common items—they become magical!

Ritual
BLESSED SALT

Making blessed salt is much easier than you might think, and no, you don't have to be a priest to bless things. Simply take a white or glass bowl and fill it with salt. Then make the sign of the cross over it three times and recite either the Hail Mary or Psalm 23 while close enough for your breath to touch it. Finish by letting three drops of holy water fall on top. Voilà, you have blessed salt. You may modify this ritual and substitute the names or symbols of your path or tradition as you see fit.

Ritual
BLESSED WATER

To make blessed water, fill a white or glass bowl with cool water. Make the sign of the cross over it three times, and then recite either the Hail Mary or Psalm 23 close enough for your breath to touch the surface. Add three *small* pinches of blessed salt and say a prayer over the water, asking that it bless everything it touches and purify all things of evil. You may modify this ritual and substitute the names and symbols of your own path or tradition as you see fit.

Ritual

BLESSED NAILS

Nails are very potent tools to have in your magical arsenal. For the purposes of this work, the best way to go about blessing and empowering them is through fire and water. To begin, place your nails in a heat-safe vessel and pour a little rubbing alcohol or Florida water over them. Not too much—just enough to get them wet. Carefully drop a match in so that they ignite. As they burn, pray the Our Father. Once they've gone out and have had a few moments to cool, I carefully move them into a glass vessel that I have filled with holy water. While they soak, I pray the Hail Mary. Once you've done that, you can lay them out on a towel to dry. After that, they are ready to use. Place them in a white bag to store them until you need them.

Boundary Spells

I was once called to a home where a negative entity kept showing up as an old, twisted man. He had been harassing a four-year-old girl, and she had been telling her parents about the scary man who liked to pinch her. After I banished him, I set up a boundary around the home to block his return. Shortly after I left, the little girl told her parents that she could see the man standing out in the street, tapping on the barrier and asking to come back in. After a week of that, he left for good. Learning to protect a property from entities is essential to this work. Once a spirit has been removed, they will often try to come back. Proper warding and border reinforcement is quite easy and is a skill each of you will need to learn. Below are my methods, as well as some advice and considerations for this work.

Creating the Boundary

To set a boundary, you'll need to combine mental magic with physical objects that act as anchors. These objects can be anything from plain rocks and garden gnomes to fancy crystals and spell jars. Simply utilizing strong intention and visualization alone, you can still protect the space for up to a few months. These boundaries are good for protecting against wayward negative energy and can keep an entity at bay when cast correctly. Adding in the anchor points, especially ones that have their own protective energy, can fortify these walls, making them stronger, and they can last indefinitely. Remember to work in a clockwise direction when creating boundaries. We'll discuss three methods below that will offer varying degrees of protection.

Psychic Boundaries

Setting up psychic boundaries is the easiest to do, but they are also the weakest. These are accomplished by grounding yourself (see page 10) and then walking the perimeter of the property three times, visualizing the barrier you want to build. This can be anything, but I suggest you go with a very sturdy, wall-like visualization, such as bricks; even simply seeing the air solidifying around the home into a dense protective dome can really help. As you do this, you want to be sure to really focus and push the energy into the walls to charge them with psychic energy. This will keep the home protected from everyday issues like random spirits floating by, bad energy, and minor spells. It may not stand up to an active attack, but it will hold nicely against low-level disturbances.

Soft Boundaries

Adding water, smoke, or powders to a psychic boundary can help feed and fortify the structure. This gives it more energy, more body, and more longevity. If you are using smoke, waters, or powders, I recommend taking these around the perimeter three times while visualizing building a wall, but we'll discuss each of the possible methods below.

If you are using waters, I recommend using holy water, salt water, moon water, or an infusion created by boiling herbs like rue, blackberry, devil's shoestring, or bay in water. Keeping tinctures on hand is helpful for this, as a couple of droppers in a bowl of water creates a similar substance. This water can be sprinkled on the ground as you walk around the perimeter of the property three times while visualizing the protective wall being built.

Other times, you may choose to use smoke. Special incense blends, resins, and herbs release a powerful spiritual vibration when burned. We can utilize these to feed the boundary and lend special properties to it. I recommend using things like premade protective incense blends from a trusted source, resins like frankincense and dragon's blood, and powerful protective plants like rue, vervain, and pine. I recommend a combination of rue, vervain, and dragon's blood that you've prayed over or charged with protective energy, but feel free to experiment. Take this incense around the home three times while visualizing a protective barrier being built.

Another option is using powders, such as a premade Fiery Wall of Protection powder, chalk, or red brick dust. If you use these options, I highly recommend praying over them or charging them with strong protective energies before using them. Once you do that, simply walk around the perimeter of the home three times while leaving a faint trail of the powder behind you to mark the boundary.

Beyond these options, you may use physical objects to mark the boundaries by placing them in the four corners. These act as anchors—a little bit like tent spikes—to hold the larger spell in place. These can be everyday objects like garden gnomes if you need to be discreet, but I have some favorites that I like to turn to. The first are river rocks. Their energy is heavy, making them a great choice to hold down the spell, and their sturdy nature lends itself to the spell. They don't have to be very big—something about the size of your fist will work nicely—and you can paint them with symbols if you'd like. If you want something fancier, you may use protective stones like obsidian, tourmaline, citrine, or quartz that has been programmed for protection and place them in the four corners. Use these in the same way, by walking around the perimeter while visualizing a protective boundary and placing them with strong intention.

If crystals and stones aren't your thing, you can always nail the spell down. You can go about this in one of two ways, using either old rusty spikes or the foot-long steel nails that you find at the hardware store. Both will get the job done, but I handle them slightly differently. Both will need to be blessed by fire. To do this, place four nails or spikes into a heat-safe vessel and pour either rubbing alcohol or Florida water over them—not too much, just enough to get them wet. Then carefully light them with a match. You may say prayers or incantations while you do this. I personally like to read Psalm 91 aloud while they burn. Once they are done, feed the rusty spikes whiskey to get them activated, or feed the nails holy water. Take one of these to each of the four corners of the property and pound them into the ground like you mean it. As you go, envision them holding a protective boundary in place.

Ritual

SETTING A HARD BOUNDARY

This ritual is saved for when you really mean business and need something very sturdy to protect the home.

You'll need four anchors of your choosing, a powder or water of your choosing, and incense of your choosing.

Pick any corner of the property to start in, and gather your tools there on the ground, inside the boundary but out of the way. Begin by grounding yourself, and place the first anchor with strong intention that the spell has begun. Walk clockwise along the perimeter to the next corner while visualizing or feeling the wall building alongside you as you go. It's important to feel that these anchor points are connected to each other every time you set one. Place the next three stones in the same manner and continue walking until you are back where you started. At that point, pick up the incense and walk the same perimeter, imagining the smoke wrapping around the property and encircling it in protection. Then finish with the powder or the water in the same manner. This means three full clockwise rectangles, each one strengthening and setting the spell. This can also be done along the inside edge of an apartment.

Ritual

THE CIRCLE OF FIRE

This is a variation of the boundary spell above, but instead of using a rectangular boundary, it uses a circle, which can be nice for smaller spaces and properties. Begin by sprinkling something like Fiery Wall powder (see Recipes section below) in a circle around the home (or along the baseboards of an apartment) in a clockwise fashion. Once you are done, set it by lighting either a white, red, or black candle and walking that same circle three times, each time imagining a fiery wall being built up around the space and making it stronger and stronger with each pass. Once you've made three circles, take the candle into the home, where you will let it burn all the way down, allowing the flame to feed the spell.

Boundaries from a Distance

Sometimes you won't be able to physically go to the home, or you'll need something that will hold up in a pinch until you can get to a location. This is when a distance spell comes in handy! Both of these can be used on location as well.

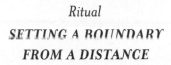

Ritual

SETTING A BOUNDARY
FROM A DISTANCE

This one is great for a quick but effective barrier and is helpful for spaces like apartments that don't necessarily have an "outside perimeter."

You'll need a drawing or photo of the apartment, home, or property as seen from above, one red candle, black pepper, and incense, such as dragon's blood.

To begin, set the drawing or photo down on a heat-safe surface and place the candle in the center of the paper, directly on top of the home; feel free to use a holder if you need one. With strong intention, light the candle and sprinkle the black pepper around the home in a clockwise circle. As you do this, say prayers or words of power stating that you are blocking the path of evil. Next, take the incense and begin to slowly pass it in a circle around the candle in a clockwise manner. See the smoke creating a wall around the home that becomes stronger with each pass. As you begin to feel the spell gain power, speed up your circles and gain momentum, feeling the power grow and the boundary begin to spin, becoming more powerful with every pass. Continue this until you feel you have reached peak power, and then set the incense aside and declare that the space is sealed off and protected. Let the candle burn all the way out.

Ritual

FIERY WALL OF PROTECTION SPELL

Not long ago, I worked a case in which a spirit had taken a particular liking to one female resident in the home who was trying to move out. It began harassing her almost daily with little touches, pokes, and pinches and made it clear that it wanted to keep her in the home. She had been suffering many delays and strange accidents and even legal red tape when trying to move out. I wasn't able to get to her, so I used this spell from afar, and it worked like a charm.

You'll need one white stick candle, four white tealight candles, four blessed nails, Fiery Wall powder (see Recipes section), Fiery Wall oil (see Recipes section), frankincense incense, a carving tool, and a white plate.

To begin, light the incense and cleanse the candles in its smoke. On the white stick candle, carve a protective symbol. On the back, carve the person's name who needs protection. Dress it with the Fiery Wall oil and charge it with your intention. Affix this candle to the center of the white plate. Dress each of the four tealights with Fiery Wall oil and a light dusting of Fiery Wall powder and arrange them around the stick candle in a cross pattern: above, below, left, and right. Place the blessed nails between the tealights with the points facing outward. Light the center candle, which represents you or the person who needs protection, and state that they are protected. Then light each of the tealights, starting at the top, then going to the bottom, then left, and then right. As you do this, declare protection from all four directions, as well as in between. Pray the Saint Michael protection prayer over it (see Prayers section), and let all candles burn all the way out.

Other Distance Spells

I *always* prefer to be on-site when I do this work. It's a lot easier, and I can get a better feel for what is going on. However, after COVID-19 hit, it became clear that I would have to develop some distance techniques. These are ones that I have used and found quite effective for times when I'm unable to physically go to the home.

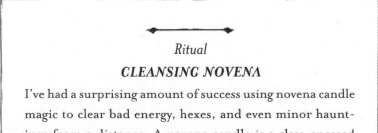

Ritual
CLEANSING NOVENA

I've had a surprising amount of success using novena candle magic to clear bad energy, hexes, and even minor hauntings from a distance. A novena candle is a glass-encased pillar candle, sometimes called a "seven-day candle" or a "vigil candle." Like most of the work in this book, this method is deceptively simple.

You'll need one white novena candle, rosemary, your preferred cleansing oil (such as garlic oil), cleansing incense, and a picture of the home you are cleansing.

Cleanse the candle and open three tunnels into the wax from the top down, using a metal tool such as a skewer or a screwdriver. These holes just help get the oil farther down into the candle. Bless the candle with a prayer or words of intention, and then pour a little oil in—not too much, just enough to get down into the holes and thinly coat the surface. Then lightly sprinkle the dried rosemary into the candle. Don't overdo it, and don't crowd the base of the wick. The point is to season the candle, not create a fire hazard. To finish, say a prayer or incantation that states what you need the candle to accomplish, and then hold it in your hands while visualizing it growing bright with white light. Set the candle on top of the picture of the home, light it along with the incense, and watch the magic happen. For best results, come back to it every day that it burns and say a prayer or incantation for cleansing and healing.

Ritual

SAINT MICHAEL NOVENA

In the case of an entity haunting (see chapter 10), you'll want to use something a little stronger. I've had great success working with Saint Michael the Archangel under these circumstances. He is an immensely powerful spirit who is especially adept at helping with protection as well as exorcism-type work. This novena ritual is a way of asking for his intercession. In this work, we aren't doing anything; we are simply asking that he help us, and he is usually happy to oblige. A novena is a series of prayers performed over a number of days while a candle burns. It's a way of showing devotion and petitioning a saint for help.

You'll need one red novena candle, granulated garlic, bay leaves, frankincense incense, Saint Michael oil (or Fiery Wall oil), a heat-safe vessel, and a picture of the home.

Begin by cleansing your novena candle and stabbing three holes in the top with a metal skewer or small screwdriver. This isn't necessarily a magical act; it just helps get the oil down into the candle. Pour in a little of the oil, just enough to get into the holes and lightly coat the top. Sprinkle in the garlic, which is sacred to Saint Michael, as well as some crushed-up dried bay, which symbolizes victory over evil. Hold the candle and visualize it glowing with bright red light, and when you're ready, pray the Saint Michael prayer (see Prayers section) and state your petition that he remove all negative entities from the home. Once that is done, place the candle on top of the picture and light it along with the incense. The candle is an offering of light and warmth to Saint Michael and is used to draw his attention. The frankincense is also an offering to sweeten the deal. If you don't have frankincense, burn bay leaves as an offering. Every day that the candle is burning, come back to it and say the Saint Michael prayer as well as a prayer that reiterates your request. If the problem you are facing is really bad, you may want to burn three of these in a row, starting the next candle just before the previous one completely goes out, to keep the work "hot."

Charms

This section centers around crafting magically charged physical objects that protect against the otherworld.

Ritual

WITCH BOTTLE

The witch bottle is an old favorite. It's what is known as a "decoy charm," meaning it carries the same energy signature as you (or the client), so anything looking for you will find the charm instead.

You'll need one bottle or jar with a lid, assorted sharps (nails, screws, pins, needles—the rustier, the better), apotropaic plants (like rue or rosemary), and personal concerns (like hair, fingernails, or blood).

Begin by adding the sharps to the jar and saying a prayer or incantation over them. Ask that they destroy any harmful energy or spirits that are sent your way. Next, pray or say an incantation over the herbs, and ask that they send the harmful energy or spirits far away. Add in the personal concerns, and then urinate into the jar, filling it all the way up to just below the rim. This part is important; folks will tell you to use vinegar or stale beer, but nothing works as good as urine. (Remember, the urine and personal concerns should belong to the person you are trying to protect.) Carefully seal the bottle and either bury it in the front yard or hide it somewhere in the home. Any bad spells or spirits that come sniffing around will find a nasty surprise. If doing this for a family, make one for each person.

Ritual

SPIRIT BOTTLE TRAP

This is another decoy charm, this time with the intent of capturing a wayward spirit. There are many ways of making a spirit bottle trap; this is my method.

You'll need one bottle (preferably blue, but work with what you've got), Spanish moss, poppy seeds, and bait (see below).

To begin, take your clean, empty bottle and add your bait. The bait you choose depends on the purpose of the trap. Do you live in a place with a lot of spirit traffic that you're looking to mitigate? If so, you can add some beer or whiskey to the bottle—just an inch or two, not much. If, however, there are spirits being sent to you or otherwise coming after you specifically, add your urine and some fingernails. This way, when they are looking for you, they'll find the bottle. Once you've added your bait, add poppy seeds. These help to sedate the spirit. Other alternatives include black mustard. Once that has been added, stuff Spanish moss inside, on top of the bait. This will ensnare them so they can't get back out. Other folks like to use nails and pins to hold them in place, but I find the moss is effective and less cruel. Leave this bottle open near your front door. It is said that the bottle will make a sudden whooshing or popping sound when it's caught something.[4] Either way, you should check it regularly by coming to stand

4. Khi Armand, *Clearing Spaces: Inspirational Techniques to Heal Your Home* (New York: Sterling Publishing, 2017), 60–62.

beside it and grounding and protecting yourself. Reach out with your hand and feel around the bottle. Does it feel full or heavy? Is something stirring inside? If there is, carefully close the bottle and dispose of it. Your method of disposal may depend on what kind of spirit you feel you've caught. Traditionally, you'd place these bottles in a fire—be careful, they explode—but if the spirit inside is particularly ornery, you could toss it in a dumpster several miles from your home. If you feel you have caught an innocent wayward spirit, you may wish to gently uncork the bottle and quickly bury it under a tree in a cemetery, with prayers that the spirit finally find peace. It's believed that the tree's branches will help transport the spirit up to the next place.

Mental Magic

As you should know by now, you can move mountains with a little visualization, intention, and will. Here are a couple of tricks that I've picked up that come in handy.

Exercise

THE FLOATING WARD

Usually, wards require a physical object that acts as an anchor, holding it in place. However, even without a physical object, you can ward a space. It doesn't last as long, but it will do in a pinch to block the path of evil. To do this, ground and stand firmly in front of where you'd like to place the ward. Then, with the index finger of your dominant hand, draw a protective or repellant symbol, such as a banishing pentagram, a cross, a rune, or a sigil. As you do this, see your fingertip leaving a trail of brilliant silver-white light. Once the symbol is finished, give it a nice tap to activate it. See it burning bright with white-hot light that shines in the direction you want it facing. This should hold anywhere from a few hours to a week or more, depending on how much you put into it.

Exercise

PILLARS OF LIGHT

This visualization can be really helpful when shifting stubborn energy from low and dark to high and bright. This can also be used to protect certain areas. To do this, stand firm and ground yourself. See a thin tendril of white light rising up from the floor toward the ceiling. See it reaching higher and higher, up past the roof. You begin to see an identical tendril floating down from the sky. See them connect, and when they do, they burst forth into a solid pillar of brilliant white light. This pillar is beautiful and pulses with waves of light that fill the space and push out all negative or stagnant energy. You may place one or many of these throughout the home. To make it more permanent, I recommend seeing a holy figure or deity descending from the sky into the pillar, where they stay. Ask them to protect the space and keep it pure.

◄————————►

Exercise

BINDING A SPIRIT

When faced with an aggressive or particularly scary spirit, it may help to bind them with this simple trick. It may not last long, but it will buy you some time. All you really need to do is get a clear picture of the spirit in your mind to start. Once you have that, reach out your hands and make a motion like you are tying them up. As you do this, see brilliant ribbons of white light wrapping around the spirit. When you feel you've crossed over them enough times, pull the ribbons tight and then tie them off. This will at least slow the spirit down.

Recipes

Sometimes potions, oils, and brews are some of your best allies in this work! Here are a few of my favorite recipes to add to your magical arsenal.

Fiery Wall Oil

This oil is used when you need powerful protection that bites. This not only blocks the path of evil, but it actively wounds the attacking force as well.

You'll need rue, red pepper flakes, angelica root, a mason jar, and sunflower oil.

Add two spoonfuls of each herb to the mason jar, and then fill it the rest of the way up with the oil. Let this steep for at least a week while routinely burning red candles on top of the jar and praying the Saint Michael prayer over it (see Prayers section) until you feel it's done. (I usually let them sit from new moon to full moon.) Use this oil carefully, and remember that there are hot peppers in there; don't get it in the eyes or on sensitive areas. Also, do not handle rue if you are pregnant or trying to become pregnant.

Fiery Wall Powder

This is the powder version of the oil recipe above, and it's used for the same purpose. This can be used to encircle candles or lay down lines of protection. Do not inhale this powder, get it in your eyes, or apply it to the body. I usually handle this with gloves.

You'll need three parts rue, two parts cayenne (powdered), two parts angelica root, half part sulfur powder (optional), and one part cornstarch.

Combine the above ingredients in a coffee grinder and blend until finely powdered. I keep a coffee grinder that is specifically for magical use that is separate from my regular grinder. Some of these ingredients, particularly sulfur, can be toxic and shouldn't be transferred to food or beverages. Use this powder to dust doorways, lay down boundaries, and dress candles.

Cut and Clear Oil

My Cut and Clear oil is specially formulated to clear harmful energetic attachments. This includes the "cords" that form between two people who become attached to one another, as well as energetic attachments such as spirit entities.

You'll need hyssop, angelica root, nine broom straws, lemon essential oil, sunflower oil, and scissors or a knife.

Combine two spoonfuls of each plant in a mason jar, along with the nine broom straws. Fill the jar the rest of the way with sunflower oil and dropper in lemon essential oil until it is scented to your liking. At this point, I like to dip a knife or an open pair of scissors into the oil three times as a way of imparting their severing power to the oil. Let the oil steep for three weeks, and burn white or yellow candles on top of the jar regularly until it's finished.

Cleansing Spray

There will be times when you are unable to use smoke to cleanse a home. When this happens, I recommend leaning on sprays. They can be very effective, and keeping some on hand can be really helpful.

You'll need one handful of fresh pine needles, fresh rosemary, the peel of one lemon, vodka or gin, and eucalyptus essential oil.

Begin by saying a prayer over all your materials. Roughly chop the plant matter, place the bits in a mason jar, and fill it to the top with the alcohol. Let this infuse for at least three weeks. When you are done, strain the liquid into a spray bottle, through either a fine sieve or cheesecloth. To this, add three to ten drops of eucalyptus essential oil. Don't go overboard; it's a very strong scent. Shake before using. You may also add a splash of holy water to the mix if you are looking for an extra kick.

The Virgin Margarita Bath

This is a bath I recommend you *always* do when you get home from doing any sort of paranormal work, and it can be helpful to prescribe to clients as well. It really gives a good energetic scrub, and it's easy to make.

You'll need sea salt, two limes, holy water, and a bathtub or a bucket.

To the bath or bucket, add three heaping spoonfuls of salt. Slice one of the limes in half and squeeze the juice directly into the bath water. Slice the other lime into thin circles and toss them into the water. You may also add a splash of holy water or Florida water.

Soak in this for ten to twenty minutes, being sure to fully immerse yourself at least once. Or, if you're using a bucket, pour it over the top of your head and scrape yourself in a downward fashion with your hands. In both cases, give the plants permission to thoroughly cleanse your mind, body, and soul energies.

Prayers

Prayers connect us directly with the Divine so that they may hear of our struggles. Through prayer, we can reach out to holy spirits or beloved deities and ask them to assist us, protect us, and guide us. Here you will find some traditional prayers as well as some of my own creation.

Guardian Angel Prayer

We all have a guardian angel, and they are ready for action in every instance of your life. Since they are so close to us already, they are often the easiest to work with for protection. I like to use the following prayer:

> *"Holy guardian angel, divine spirit that walks beside me all the days of my life, I seek your help and ask that you block the path of evil. Preserve me against every danger and keep me safe in my work. Amen."*

Hail Mary

The Hail Mary is an old favorite for calling in the Divine Mother. I pull this one out for just about everything from blessing charms and ritual tools to driving out evil spirits. This prayer evokes the presence of Mary, Mother of God, a powerful protector and benevolent mother. The traditional version is as follows:

"Hail Mary, full of grace, the Lord is with thee. Blessed are you among women, and blessed is the fruit of your womb, Jesus Christ. Hail Mary, Mother of God, pray for us sinners now and at the hour of our death. Amen."

A lot of modern folks who have been drawn to pray the rosary over the last several years have begun to say this prayer with a looser adherence to the traditional version, thus creating alternatives that you can use, such as:

"Hail Mary, full of light, the Lord is with thee. Blessed are you among women, and blessed is the fruit of your womb. Hail Mary, Mother of God, protect your children now and in every instance of our lives. Amen."

Our Father

The Our Father, much like the Hail Mary, can be used for just about everything, including blessing and protection. This is how we summon the Divine Father. The traditional version is as follows:

"Our Father, who art in heaven, hallowed be thy name. Thy kingdom come, thy will be done, on earth as it is in heaven. Give us this day our daily bread, and forgive us our trespasses, as we forgive those who trespass against us. And lead us not into temptation, but deliver us from evil. Amen."

Saint Michael Prayers

Saint Michael the Archangel is a powerful spirit who aims to protect the innocent, dole out justice, and fight off evil forces. These two prayers are used to evoke his presence and protection. The first is the most common, and I recommend using this when facing off against malicious spirits:

"Saint Michael the Archangel, defend us in battle. Be our protection against the wickedness and snares of the devil. May God rebuke him, we humbly pray; and do thou, O Prince of the Heavenly Host, by the power of God, cast into hell Satan and all the evil spirits who prowl the world seeking the ruin of souls. Amen."

The second prayer is one of my own creation, but I like the symbolism and feeling it brings:

"Blessed Saint Michael the Archangel, faithful servant of God, encase me in your holy shield. Let me be like holy metal, impervious to danger and evil. Defend me with your flaming sword and surround me with the holy fires of God. With you I am safe. Amen."

CHAPTER 12
Portals, Doorways, and Highways

Portals exist and are more common than most folks think. Identifying whether you have a portal or not is imperative if you are trying to dispel the activity. After all, you can't get rid of houseguests while you're inviting more in. Portals are often identified by random and inconsistent activity. For instance, if your activity is always the old man who smokes cigars, well, you probably don't have a portal. However, if one day it's the man who smokes, and then it's the lady in white, and then there are goblin creatures, and then those go away but other spirits arrive, you may have a portal. If they seem to be coming and going and the activity is broad and inconsistent, this generally points to an open doorway in the home that will need to be closed.

These doorways come in three main varieties: ones that pour into a home, ones that pour out of a home, and ones that go both ways. Usually, the ones that only lead out of the home aren't as easy to notice, because they are much less dramatic. They do draw in some activity, because spirits will look for them as a means of transportation, but the activity is usually fleeting. Portals that spill into the home are often much more chaotic, as the activity tends to pile up over time as more and more things arrive. Some will leave, but depending on the home, others may choose to stay. The portals that go in both directions tend to reach an equilibrium, with as many spirits leaving as arriving, but it can still be quite chaotic with all the coming and going.

Before doing any work to resolve the haunting, you should check to see if you have any portals. Ones that spill out of the home may be left open until the end, as they provide a convenient exit for anything nasty hanging around. Portals that pour into the home should be closed immediately or be changed to an outward-facing portal (see chapter 12). The portals that go in both directions may be capped to let things out but stop things from coming back in (see below). Another detail to note is that most portals spin like a whirlpool. Determining in which direction the portal is spinning can be quite helpful for manipulating them (more on that later).

You may also run into something we often refer to as a "spirit highway." This is a current of energy that spirits can use for faster or easier transportation. I always describe it as something akin to those conveyor belts in the floors of airports that you can step on to either carry you or speed you up when you are in a hurry. These highways can be created by all kinds of things, but some of the common culprits include underground water and historical usage of the land. In the case of underground water, energy flows with water, so occasionally underground rivers or streams will create a spirit highway aboveground. Homes with this type of water running below them may receive frequent activity. Alternatively, if a road went through a piece of property for a substantial period of time, the energy still remains long after it is gone, and it may produce a spirit highway. Same goes for areas a railroad used to run through.

I'm going to walk you through the methods I use for dealing with portals. These are techniques that are designed to be used without tools. When you are in the field, you won't always have access to a specific candle, plant, or stone. You'll have to learn to work the magic using just yourself. Always make sure you are grounded before attempting any of these. This will help ensure that you don't overload yourself.

Exercise

CREATING A SEAL

We are going to start simple and work our way up. To begin, I will teach you to create a seal. This is a magical barrier used to contain spirits or create boundaries against them. This works best when fortifying an existing structure— meaning, this is best used to make a wall impermeable to spirits or to lock a mirror so it can't be used as a portal. It doesn't work as well if you try to create a boundary in midair without a physical structure, but it can be done.

You'll need a cup or bowl, salt, and water.

Now, don't feel the need to be fancy here. I've used tap water, a red Solo cup, and salt from a to-go packet to do this before. Work with whatever you have on hand. Mix the salt and water together in your vessel of choice and approach the surface you wish to seal. Square up to it and ground yourself, forming a clear intention in your mind about what you are about to do. Then, without breaking concentration, dip your index and middle fingers into the water, apply your fingertips to the wall, and trace a clockwise spiral, starting from the outside and winding inward toward the center. Don't lift your fingers, even if they dry up. As you do this, visualize a seal forming across the surface and pulling in toward the center of your spiral as you work, holding the tension as you go. When you get to the center of the spiral, place your two fingers or your hand in the center and press firmly. Don't press with your physical body, though; press with your *magic* and give it the command to lock. I know I've done it correctly when I hear a soft click in my head and feel the surface lock beneath my hand. Usually, this feels like a ripple or a shudder. This can be done to lock walls, floors, ceilings, and mirrors.

Sometimes you need to do this to a doorway to keep spirits from entering or exiting a place. Please use these seals judiciously and only when necessary. Trapping spirits is not only mean, it's often a dangerous gamble, because if they get free they're likely to seek revenge. But sometimes all you can do is temporarily corral them while you come up with a plan B.

To begin, you'll make the salt water like you normally do, but instead of making the spiral on the door, you'll want to go around the doorframe in a clockwise direction, starting at the bottom left side of the frame and going up and over the top and coming down the right side. At that point, I rewet my fingers and draw a line across the threshold left to right, completing the circuit. Do this last part like you mean it. You're drawing a boundary. I do this with the door closed, and once I've completed the circuit, I dunk my whole right hand in the salt water, place it flat on the center of the door, and press like before. When I hear the click and feel the surface lock, I then turn the doorknob with my left hand and knock three times with my right. On the third knock, I let the door swing open with my left hand and step back, releasing the spell. If done correctly, the barrier will hold, and you should be able to feel the invisible membrane sealing the threshold. These will hold indefinitely. Creating a seal takes some practice, but you'll get the hang of it.

Exercise

CLOSING A PORTAL

In a pinch, creating a seal will provide a temporary solution to portals. However, even though a seal will hold for quite a while, it lacks finality—a bit like boarding the portal up with plywood instead of pouring cement. When we close a portal, we are removing it from existence completely. This does not require any tools, but if you'd prefer to use a wand or an athame, you can do that as well.

To begin, locate the portal and stand in front of it. Most portals will be on walls, so they are usually vertical. Reach out your hand and try to feel how big the portal is. I find they are often quite large—between three and six feet in diameter—and circular in nature. You may find smaller ones the size of portholes, but those are less common. Use your hand and psychic senses to feel around the edges of the portal and get a sense for its outer boundaries. Once you find the outer edges, you can go about this in a couple of ways, and I recommend you use the method that makes the most sense for you. In either method, you'll need to ground yourself and then form your intention clearly; something like, "I close this portal through all timelines and dimensions," will work just fine.

The first method requires you to grab the outer edges of the portal with both hands on opposite sides (for example, the three o'clock and nine o'clock positions). With strong will and visualization, slowly pull your hands together, imagining the portal shrinking smaller and smaller until you get to the center. At that point, place your dominant hand on the center and press the same way you did when you made the seal. Again, you should hear or feel a click like a lock or receive some other indication that it is complete.

The second method is done much the same way as the seal, in which you find the outer edges of the portal and then, using your dominant hand, begin to make a clockwise spiral. Start on the outside and move your way in. As you do this, see the portal spiraling inward and tightening with every revolution until you get to the center. At this point, you again place your dominant hand in the center and press with strong will and intention to seal the portal through all timelines and dimensions, thus wiping it from existence. I prefer this method myself.

Sometimes you will find portals lying across the ground horizontally. They tend to feel like large drains, and they will cause the energy above them to spin, causing folks to feel nauseated, dizzy, or otherwise disoriented. To close these, I like to use a pendulum. First, I stand where I feel the center of the portal is. I let the pendulum hang freely and ask it to show me in which direction the portal is spinning. Sometimes you don't even have to ask; sometimes the pendulum will just begin moving on its own, due to the current of energy caused by the portal. Also, some portals will be so strong you can feel it yourself. Once you've determined in which direction the portal is spinning, you can close it. Make sure you are grounded, and set a strong, clear intention. Then begin swinging the pendulum in the opposite direction. It may take a little extra effort, as the current of the portal will create some drag, but continue on. Eventually, you'll feel the spin of the portal begin to slow, and it will finally come to a complete stop. You may feel or hear a click as it balances itself and comes to rest.

Exercise

REVERSING THE CURRENT

When you come across a portal that flows only one way—either into or out of the home—it's sometimes helpful to switch the direction the portal is facing. For instance, if you find a portal that is flowing into the home, you may want to flip it so that it flows out of the home to give the spirits a quick and easy exit. There are two methods I use for this. The first is my preferred method, but use whichever makes the most sense to you.

To begin, ground yourself and square up to the portal as usual. Form a clear intention for what you are about to do—change the direction of the portal—and then reach out with your dominant hand and feel for the edge of the portal. When you find the edge, use your powerful will to grab hold of it and spin the portal like a revolving door. Give it a good shove, because they tend to be heavy. It may spin rather fast at first, but it will slowly come to a stop, facing the other direction. If you still feel that it is pouring into the home, spin it again until you feel that it lands facing the opposite direction.

The second method requires a little finesse but can be quite effective. You'll want to start as before, by grounding and squaring up to the portal. You'll then need to assess in which direction the portal is spinning. Some folks will be able to feel it just by being near it. If you're unsure, ask your pendulum to show you in which direction it spins—clockwise or counterclockwise. Once you know, form your clear intention and then reach out with your dominant hand and place it in the current of the portal. Then begin to move your hand in circles going *against* the flow. Eventually, the portal will slow down and balance completely. Once it hits that point, you may stop and press to seal it, or you can keep going so that the portal will begin to pick up speed going in the opposite direction and thus reversing the current. Once it gets back up to normal speed, release it, and it should hold.

Exercise

ONE-WAY CAP

When you have a bidirectional portal (one that flows in both directions at once), it's often helpful to turn it into a unidirectional portal (one that flows in only one direction). For instance, if you have a portal flowing both in and out of the home, it is wise to block off part of it so that things can still escape but nothing else can come in. Otherwise, your attempts at clearing the home will be futile.

To do this, you'll want to begin by locating the portal, grounding, and squaring up to it. Form your strong intention and take a deep breath. With force, project a mental image of a protective symbol over the portal. It should be big enough to cover the whole opening, and it should be facing away from you into the portal. (This is if you are wanting to make sure nothing comes in but things can go out; if for some reason you want to make sure nothing goes out but things can come in, you'd flip it in the other direction so that it's facing you.) I often use flaming pentagrams that blaze forth into the portal, turning away anything that may try to come through. These hold indefinitely, depending on your strength as a caster.

Exercise

OPENING A PORTAL

Opening a single transport portal is very simple, but you must do so carefully. Opening portals can be a dangerous game if you aren't clear about what you are doing or what you're allowing. All you really need to do is ground yourself and set a clear intention. With this intention, it's important to decide things like: Where does the portal go? How big is it? How long will it stay open? Once you have a precise intention, extend your dominant hand in the direction of where you'd like to place the portal. With strong will and visualization, see the air spiraling in like a drain, opening the portal to wherever you'd like it to go. You may begin to feel a gentle pull in that direction.

Exercise

BYPASSING A SPIRIT HIGHWAY

Sometimes you will find a spirit highway running straight through the home, and there is not much you can do about it. Most of the time, these create chronic mild activity that most folks can live with. However, if it becomes disruptive, you may need to address the issue. While you can't necessarily get rid of or permanently block off a spirit highway, you can reorganize it. This process takes some time, a clear plan, and a little imagination, but it can be done.

To begin, assess the flow of the highway: In which direction does it seem to be flowing? What areas of the house does it seem to be crossing through? How wide is it? These are all things that you'll likely be able to sense, or you can use your pendulum to determine the details. Once you have a clear picture of the spirit highway, ground yourself and form a clear intention. What you are going to do is essentially cut the spirit highway at two places: once on either side of the home, where the flow enters and where it exits. You'll then be lifting the corridor up above the house. I find it's easier to lift it straight up because there it will still be in line with the flow of the energy. It's much harder to move it to the left or the right, out of the natural path. This way, the highway continues as normal but simply goes over the home instead of through it. In the places where you cut the stream of energy, be sure to open portals that will send them up to the higher level and then back down once they cross to the other side. This way, as the spirits come through, they sort of just pop up to the upper level and then back down through the portals. Most of the time, the spirits don't even notice.

CHAPTER 13
Working with Clients

Before you go, let's talk about the people you will work with. We must remember that at the end of the day, this is a customer service job, and you'll find there are certain archetypes, conversations, and obstacles you'll routinely come up against. Here we will discuss some of these, as well as general advice for handling these common situations with grace and dignity. My best advice is to always remain calm and remember that you are the one steering the ship. These events can be rather chaotic, and having a strong voice of reason to put things in order is invaluable.

Client Archetypes

When doing this work, you will quickly realize that you are seeing some of the same characters over and over again. Though no case is the same, the types of people you meet will begin to fit a bit of a pattern, and they each will need to be worked with differently.

The Family Skeptic

The one who causes investigators the most anxiety is the family skeptic. This role is normally played by the oldest male in the home, though there are some exceptions. They can be quite intimidating, but I've rarely found them to be outright disruptive. This person will most likely self-identify as "the family skeptic" or otherwise make it noticeably clear. They can seem like a big, immovable boulder, but in my experience, these are highly misunderstood people.

You may be surprised to find that often these folks have experienced the most supernatural phenomena out of anyone in the house. They simply feel like they can't speak about it, for one of two reasons. The first is that they feel they have to remain the "sane one" or feel their role in the family structure dictates that they can't believe or discuss what's happening. They see themselves as a great anchor of the family whose job is to keep everyone steady. Due to this, they feel it's their job to oppose the current dominant household belief in an attempt to regain balance. The second reason is that they are scared shitless and the only thing keeping them together is the vehement denial that anything supernatural exists. If they accept that it exists, then they have to accept that they may be in danger, and that's something they are unable to handle. Usually, I find the family skeptic to have a combination of both of these going on. The reason why this often falls to the oldest male in the family is due to the overwhelming feeling of powerlessness these situations can cause. Most men in the home feel they have to be protectors, and many in this role will have some sort of plan in the back of their mind should they ever have to defend their family against intrusion. But what if the intruder isn't a person but a spirit? How do they defend against that? For them, a haunting is the result of their failure to protect their family.

The best way to bring this particular archetype around to your side is to create a safe space. I recommend trying to crack this nut during the initial in-person interview. After they spend some time listening to the stories from the rest of the family and getting to know that you are not some wack job there to con them out of their money, they begin to relax. If they open up about something, gently welcome them to say more by expressing genuine curiosity, but without making a big deal out of it. From there, they will often take the reins, become a little softer, and open up nicely.

The Chatty Ones

Usually, when someone contacts you about a haunting, you are the first and only person they've really been able to speak openly with about their situation. When folks experience a haunting, they often feel isolated and worry that if they tell people about what's going on, they'll be seen as "crazy" or people won't believe them. When you present yourself as a paranormal investigator, you are sending folks the message that you are a safe person to talk to about this, and that's usually when the floodgates open. Folks will get quite worked up, and you may even wonder a bit if they are in control of themselves as the stories come out. They may begin to tremble as they speak or even go careening off the subject at hand and go into childhood experiences they had, or other unrelated incidences. This can be an incredibly beautiful experience, and you can often see a very noticeable change in people as they are finally able to speak their truth at last. However, sometimes folks have bad timing, or once they begin, getting them to stop can be a bit of a chore.

To mitigate this issue, I always recommend an intake interview. This is the client's chance to get it all out. Let them know that now is their time to talk, and remind them that during the actual work appointment you'll need to be left alone. The intake interview can go on for several hours, so get comfortable. Usually, once they've been given time to say what they need to say, they are willing to leave you alone during the actual work portion. However, if they continue to be a chatterbox, I find giving them a job is helpful. Ask them to make a list of their experiences and look for commonalities while you work, or ask them to stuff small baggies with salt and herbs to protect the home once you're done. Most of the time, these tasks give them a sense of accomplishment and participation.

The Mystery Roommate

It's extremely common for folks who are experiencing hauntings to have an unfortunate houseguest. Most often, this is a person who had been down on their luck or otherwise financially compromised, and the family offered them a place to stay temporarily. As wonderful as that sentiment is, this is often where the problems begin. Not only does the temporary roommate usually turn into a permanent one, but they'll also often end up being the source of the haunting.

Given their circumstances and social politics, it's usually difficult for the family to get the guest to leave. Most commonly, I find that these types of roommates cause the haunting through untreated disorders, drug addiction, dabbling in the occult, or usually a mixture of all three. These are all things that can bring darkness into the home or attract negative entities. This isn't to say that everyone you extend a hand to is bad or will spiritually compromise your home, but this is something I've seen time and time again.

The Drama Queen

Some folks read too deeply into every little noise and omen and assume the worst. A slight breeze can become a "demon" in their minds, and a bad night of sleep can be evidence that they are being tormented by evil spirits. Even after you leave, every time their house creaks or groans, they may call you up to tell you, "It's back!" If you come across a client who is calling you routinely about innocuous things, you may need to have a conversation with them. After all, this mentality only invites things in and makes agreements like crazy. Let them know that they need to stand in their power and not give it away to every sound and feeling.

Alternatively, when folks experience paranormal activity, they often assume other folks won't believe them or will think that they are overreacting. To combat this, some folks will embellish the story of their hauntings in hopes of being taken seriously, and I don't fault them for this. Who wants to call in a team of professionals because you've heard a tapping sound at night? Folks feel that if they are going to involve professionals, they'd better have a damn good reason, and they try to provide one. In a funny attempt to legitimize their call, people will often amp up the drama level in order to not be seen as dramatic. Most of the time, it's easy to notice, and honestly all client testimony should be taken with a grain of salt. The easiest way to soothe this problem is to simply let them know that you believe them. After they know that, they tend to calm down.

Other times, though, you can run into people who utilize their hauntings as a way to get attention. They may struggle and rail against the haunting, declaring they are afraid and want to be free of it forever, but then they will turn around and go against your advice or instructions in order to prolong the haunting. If you suspect this is happening, you need to have a conversation with them. If their behavior continues in this manner, you may have to walk away from the case.

Children

Though you'll most often be working with adults, you will occasionally find yourself needing to interview children to get their take on what is happening. Please be patient with them, use common language, and avoid asking them leading questions. In this day and age, when paranormal belief is on trend, it's common for folks to take any account from children as completely factual. However, when dealing with children, it's also important to ask about things like what kind of media they are consuming: movies, TV, video games, books, and social media. These can all deeply influence how they interpret the world around them. Similarly, feelings of being unsafe in the home, or tales of a faceless entity that physically harms them, may be signs of domestic concerns. In my experience, those who are abusing their children don't often invite strangers in to investigate, so you probably won't come across this, but please keep this understanding close at hand just in case.

The Power of Tact

When working with clients, it's best to keep in mind how they may be feeling. It's easy to get desensitized in this work and forget how jarring a haunting can be for the everyday person. It's important that you communicate clearly but keep the client calm, as the more afraid they become, the more power the haunting gains.

The key is to be direct but compassionate. You need to tell them the truth about their situation, but you'll want to deliver it in a way that they can handle. Where I see this go wrong the most is when folks are delivering news about some unsavory spirits. Instead of saying, "There is a dangerous demonic entity in your home that wishes to feed off you and your family," try, "There is a presence in the home that I'm concerned about." This is an honest statement but gives you room to elaborate without causing panic. I recommend avoiding words like "evil," "demonic," and others that folks may have a preprogrammed and highly emotional response to.

Similarly, it's easy to make folks feel stupid when you use paranormal lingo, so going slow and explaining what you mean in plain English is always the best option. Also, don't be too quick to debunk, as this can also make folks feel inferior or self-conscious. If the weird whispering sound is truly coming from their dishwasher, you should tell them that, but you should also let them know that it's a common mistake or is something that startled you as well before you found the source. Even if this isn't true, it will help them keep their chin up. Again, you have to remember that if you plan to do this work professionally, it is a customer service job.

Common Obstacles

In this section, we will cover the main obstacles you are likely to come up against when working with clients. These are usually social in nature, and it's important that when you are addressing these issues, you remain polite but *firm*. These are boundaries that need to be adhered to by the clients for your safety and theirs. While you must always be cordial, remember that they hired you to do a job, and that means you (or the team leader) are the captain of this ship for as long as they need your services. If they refuse to respect these boundaries, you are well within your rights to leave without doing the work. I've only had to do so once, but the client was quick to change their behavior after I did. Let's look at some of these obstacles and their potential remedies.

The Gathering Crowd

You'll quickly find that the paranormal tends to draw a crowd. In order to do this work, you need space to concentrate. Therefore, I often ask that only one or two people be present, and I usually insist that they wait outside while I'm working. However, news that "paranormal investigators are coming" tends to spread quickly, and it's not unusual for me to arrive at a house and find the clients, their extended family, a few friends, a neighbor, their hairdresser, and even on one occasion a former teacher of theirs from elementary school. These folks are very excited to tell you about the time they saw a ghost or were abducted by a UFO. If allowed, they will follow you about the home like an entourage, gawk at you while you work, and prod you with questions. This makes it almost impossible to get any work done, and you are likely to end up just giving a seminar on the paranormal instead. While that is a wonderful educational opportunity for them, you have a job to do and people who need your help. Stay on task.

To avoid this situation, you should be clear from the start that it's important that only necessary persons be on-site while you are working. I like to let the client know this on first contact when I'm walking them through the process, and again when making the appointment to come to the house. Be sure to explain that not only does this help you do your job, it's also a safety concern. When doing a home exorcism, it is common for entities to act up, and anyone who is present could become a potential target. It's possible, if not likely, that someone could be bitten, pushed, or scratched—or worse, they could become the victim of a spirit attachment. Being transparent about the dangers tends to clear up this problem rather quickly. Still, expect to have a few tagalongs, and don't be afraid to set firm boundaries about your need for space and quiet.

The Chronic Case

You will not be able to help everyone, and it's important that you accept this fact early on. Some cases will be out of your league, and some clients will willingly sabotage your efforts. In either event, it's important to know when to back away from a case and either inform the client that you can no longer assist them or refer them to someone else. When this happens, I don't want you to get bogged down with feeling like a failure. This will happen to you and will continue to happen over your time in this work. It's just a natural part of it. Having clear honesty with yourself about your efforts and skill level is imperative to successfully doing this work.

Religious Differences

What happens if you, a witch, must help a devoutly Christian family? Do you tell them to get over it and embrace the dark goddess? Nope, you do not. It is always best to adapt to the views of the client, no matter your personal feelings. Most folks become rather open-minded once faced with a haunting, and they'll often want an education on their circumstances, so it's usually a nonissue. However, on occasion you will come up against some really deep-rooted beliefs in your clients that create barriers. Just remember, you are there to perform a job. You don't have to be their friend or agree with them in order to do this job. You just have to make it through to the end. And as a witch, you really should feel comfortable walking in all religions anyway. Adaptation is key, and if you have to change your language to fit vocabulary they understand, you should be ready to do so. Remember, part of your job is to make sure they can protect themselves after you leave. Our beliefs can be very powerful, and teaching a Christian person to use a cross and prayer to defend themselves will serve them much better than something they don't believe in, like crystals or pentagrams.

Charging Money

I get asked a lot if I charge, or how I feel about people charging money for this type of work. My honest opinion is that you should do what you feel is best in this regard. I spent many years doing this work for free on my own, and then I joined a team that does not charge either. Personally, I feel that money should not be a barrier to people getting help when supernatural issues occur. At the same time, I've also experienced how being "free help" can lead to people treating you like their own personal on-call paranormal worker and occasionally disrespecting the boundaries you place around your time and energy. If in doubt, there's nothing wrong with accepting donations or making a "preferred donation" amount known. This way, folks will be inclined to compensate you for your time and effort, but if someone needs help and doesn't have the money, it's okay. If you do charge set amounts, make sure to charge based on your experience and skill level.

Safety First

One last thing: yes, we are here to help people, but we can only do that by keeping ourselves safe. Outside of spiritual protection, you're gonna need to use the ol' noodle machine to keep yourself safe. Don't go into a stranger's house alone. Let someone know where you are going and when you plan to be back. Don't feel you need to help everyone, especially anyone that seems dangerous, unstable, or just gives you a bad feeling. Travel in pairs or in groups. If you need to check out attics, crawl spaces, or abandoned buildings, wear a mask that can filter asbestos. Don't take on cases you don't think you can handle, and be honest with yourself about your limits. Bring a water bottle and a snack; this work can take a while, and you will need to be hydrated and energized. Some entities make homes hot, too, and this can lead to dehydration more quickly than you think. Take care of yourself out there.

CONCLUSION
Before You Go ...

This is it. Are you ready? Do you have everything you need? Good, because out there beyond this page is a vast expanse of unexplored territory to discover. The world needs people like you out there doing this work. There are families with no one to turn to, people who think no one will believe them, and children making "imaginary" friends at a tea party right now as you are reading this. These things happen every day, and now you can help do something about it.

It's time to be brave. Lower your shoulders. Straighten your spine. I want you to know that I'm proud of you. As you have journeyed through this book, you've acquired new skills and a new understanding of the world on the other side. Like all things, when it comes to this work, the more you learn, the less it seems you know. I'm sure you have questions, but you'll learn more as you go. Start by checking out the bibliography that comes next and reading through the materials there. Don't forget to practice, too. I know you are nervous, but you have everything you need. You carry it with you in your ability to form an intention and will something into existence. You carry it with you here in this book, and in my voice keeping you company along the way. It's dangerous to go it alone, so I'll be here with you in these pages. Refer to them anytime you need assistance, or a friend. This work can feel very lonely. The path is long, and you can go years sometimes without crossing paths with kindred in this work.

But now, we walk this path together, and one day I'm sure we'll come across each other for real.

It's time now. Don't be scared. You're brave enough to do this. Take a deep breath, and most importantly ...

Give 'em hell.

Recommended Reading

Allen, Sue. *Spirit Release: A Practical Handbook*. Lanham, MD: John Hunt Publishing, 2010.

Armand, Khi. *Clearing Spaces: Inspirational Techniques to Heal Your Home*. New York: Sterling Publishing, 2017.

Auerbach, Loyd. *ESP, Hauntings and Poltergeists: A Parapsychologist's Handbook*. Self-published, CreateSpace Independent Publishing Platform, 2016.

Belanger, Michelle. *The Ghost Hunter's Survival Guide: Protection Techniques for Encounters with the Paranormal*. Woodbury, MN: Llewellyn Worldwide, 2010.

Clarkson, Michael. *The Poltergeist Phenomenon: An In-Depth Investigation into Floating Beds, Smashing Glass, and Other Unexplained Disturbances*. Pompton Plains, NJ: New Page Books, 2011.

Denning, Mehta, and Osborne Phillips. *The Llewellyn Practical Guide to Psychic Self-Defense & Well-Being*. Saint Paul, MN: Llewellyn Worldwide, 1983.

Penczak, Christopher. *The Witch's Shield: Protection Magick & Psychic Self-Defense*. Saint Paul, MN: Llewellyn Worldwide, 2004.

Sebastiani, Althaea. *By Rust of Nail & Prick of Thorn: The Theory & Practice of Effective Home Warding*. Self-published, 2017.

Winkowski, Mary Ann. *When Ghosts Speak: Understanding the World of Earthbound Spirits*. New York: Grand Central Publishing, 2007.

Notes

Notes